THEOLOGY OF PREACHING
Essays on Vision and Mission in the Pulpit

Theology of Preaching
Essays on Vision and Mission in the Pulpit

edited by
Gregory Heille, OP

MELISENDE

Theology of Preaching: Essays on Vision and Mission in the Pulpit

First published 2001 by
Melisende
39 Chelmsford Road
London E18 2PW
Tel. +44 (0)20 8498 9768
Fax +44 (0)20 8504 2558
E mail: melisende@cwcom.net
www.melisende.cwc.net

ISBN 1 901764 19 2

Cover monoprint: *My Body Broken*, courtesy of the artist, John Gerlach, OP

Editor: Leonard Harrow

Printed at the St Edmundsbury Press, England

CONTENTS

CONTRIBUTORS

Michael A Becker serves as diocesan Director of Vocations at the Basilica of St Michael the Archangel, Loretto, Pennsylvania, Diocese of Altoona-Johnstown.

Audrey Borschel is a lay ecclesial minister serving as Pastoral Associate at St Thomas Aquinas Parish, Indianapolis, Indiana, Archdiocese of Indianapolis.

Katherine C Calore is Assistant Rector for Youth, Children, and Families at Christ Episcopal Church, Springfield, Missouri, Episcopal Diocese of West Missouri.

Linus Ebele Edogwo, from the Archdiocese of Onitsha, Nigeria, teaches religion at St Benedict's Preparatory School and serves as Pastoral Associate at St Mary's Parish, Newark, New Jersey.

Daniel Francis, CSsR, is an itinerant preacher for the Redemptorist Missions, Bronx, New York.

James Hayes is a campus minister at St Thomas Aquinas Catholic Church and Student Center, Ames, Iowa, Archdiocese of Dubuque.

Gregory Heille, OP, is Promoter of Preaching, Dominican Province of St Albert the Great, USA, and Associate Professor of Homiletics and Director of the Doctor of Ministry in Preaching Program, Aquinas Institute of Theology, St Louis, Missouri.

Duncan Macpherson, a deacon of the Archdiocese of Westminster, was formerly Principal Lecturer in Theology and Religious Studies, St Mary's University College, Strawberry Hill, University of Surrey.

David G Morman is a chaplain at Home on the Range and Pastor of St John the Baptist Parish and St Mary Parish in Beach and Golva, North Dakota, Diocese of Bismarck.

MAKE THE SCRIPTURES RELEVANT

Gregory Heille, OP

An amazing little study on Catholic preaching in the United States of America was done by scripture scholars Barbara Reid, OP, and Leslie Hoppe, OFM, at the Catholic Theological Union, Chicago, in 1998. Though the analytical sample of Sunday homilies was statistically small, the study's results bear true to my experience as an interested observer of Catholic preaching:

> 96 percent cite the text.
> 66 percent rephrase the text.
> 16 percent explain the cultural realities of the text.
> 73 percent lead the congregation to identify with the story's characters.
> 21 percent engage the theological views of the text.
> 12 percent are aware of the text's theological pluralism.
> 81 percent show how the text illumines Christian life.
> 90 percent show how the text suggests behaviors.
> 27 percent show evidence of sound exegetical preparation.[1]

The 27 percent figure is jarring. It is indicative of the fact that though most preachers have received traditional exegetical formation in the historical critical method, they (understandably) have not found this method adequate for meaningful preaching—preaching that speaks to contemporary life. By and large, they have not learned more recent and more helpful social-scientific, reader-response, or contextual approaches to scriptural hermeneutics. Unfortunately, many (especially first-world male) preachers, receiving the skewed impression that biblical scholars have ventured willy-nilly into alien territories of postmodernism and feminism, are edgy about investigating many

---

[1] Barbara E Reid, OP, and Leslie J Hoppe, OFM, 'Preaching from the Scriptures: New Directions for Preparing Preachers' (Chicago: Catholic Theological Union, 1998), 21.

of the preacher-friendly resources being published from these hermeneutical frames of reference.

The 16 percent figure is likewise disconcerting. In a self-absorbed, individualistic culture in which the venture of religion into public life is widely regarded as the misdirection of the so-called religious right, few first-world preachers understand the systemic and cultural dynamics of text, tradition, or world. As a consequence, mainstream preachers are further hobbled as interpreters of the worlds behind and in front of the text.

The 21 and 12 percent figures suggest that even though most first-world preachers studied dogmatic theology for the duration of their ministerial formation, they have not understood or embraced a vocation to continual, communal theological reflection—the 'see-judge-act' pastoral circle of contextual theology and ministry. Without this skill and commitment, preachers cannot keep their views of God, the human person, and Jesus Christ up to date with the demands of experience.

The 96, 66, 73, 81, and 90 percent figures amply demonstrate an awareness that preaching is supposed to make a connection between Scripture and experience. Certainly, this is the most singular cry of the believers in the pew: 'Make the Scriptures relevant to my life.' Preachers stab at this, generally by taking one of two tangential approaches to the text and, for that matter, to life (in the sense, perhaps, of stopping at Riceour's 'first naivete'[2]): they tell stories, or they expostulate dogma. Lacking the critical hermeneutical and theological skills to bring the text and life into direct and authentic dialogue (Riceour's 'critical enquiry'), they fail (at least as preachers) to reach the goal of their vocation—to be 'mediators of meaning'[3] (Riceour's 'second naivete').

In this book of essays, eight preachers engage in theological reflection about preaching. As they reflect upon their considerable experience of the pulpit, you are invited to engage in critical reflection on the nature and the message of the Christian ministry of the Word.

These preachers are a fraction of the many Catholic priests, deacons,

---

[2] Mary Margaret Pazdan, OP, Professor of New Testament at Aquinas Institute of Theology, draws on the work of Loretta Dornisch to explain the Riceour methodology of interpreting Scripture by saying that *first naiveté* refers to personal experience as a horizon for interpretation, *critical inquiry* to a studied exploration of other horizons for interpretation, and *second naiveté* to re-evaluation of experience and presuppositions. The goal of meaning is achieved through personal integration and transformative communal engagement with the text. See Loretta Dornisch, 'Riceour and Biblical Research', *Faith and Philosophy in the Writings of Paul Riceour*, Problems in Contemporary Philosophy, vol. 29 (Lewiston, NY: Edwin Mellin, 1990), 265-97.

[3] See the Bishops' Committee on Priestly Life and Ministry, National Conference of Catholic Bishops, *Fulfilled in Your Hearing: The Homily in the Sunday Assembly* (Washington, DC: United States Catholic Conference, 1982), 7-8.

and lay ecclesial ministers, as well as Protestant ministers, enrolled in the Doctor of Ministry in Preaching program at Aquinas Institute of Theology, St Louis, Missouri. Aquinas Institute is a graduate school of theology and ministry in the Dominican (the Order of Preachers) tradition sponsored by the Province of St Albert the Great, USA. Ten years ago, the school chose preaching as the integrating principle of its mission and curriculum and instituted the Doctor of Ministry in Preaching program as a response to the call by the United States Bishops in 1982 for the establishment of a Catholic doctoral program in homiletics.[4] The program now celebrates its numerous graduates who are engaged in pastoral ministry, homiletic teaching, and itinerant preaching. In Catholic theological education, the program is one of a kind.

The Catholic Church in the United States certainly has changed in the twenty years since the United States Bishops' Conference promulgated *Fulfilled in Your Hearing: The Homily in the Sunday Assembly.* As baptized disciples engage in full, conscious, and active participation in apostolic and ecclesial life and as the presbyterate is shaken on several fronts by a sense of radical diminishment, the ministry of the Word has diversified. Today's gospel-actualized community calls into play a panoply of ministries of the Word: *catechesis* in Christian formation, *paraclesis* (if I might be permitted to search for a word) in pastoral care, *evangelization of culture* (an expression of popes Paul VI and John Paul II) in action for justice, and of course, at the summit and source of ecclesial life, *homilia* (*homily*)—preaching in the liturgical assembly. As I say elsewhere, 'The mission of the preacher, therefore, according to his or her ministerial position in the community, is to attend to the gospel actualization of the community—in its aspects of pastoral care, Christian formation, action for justice, and worship.'[5]

When I explain to people that I 'teach preaching', I often am greeted by a quizzical stare. The fact is that many Catholic preachers received no homiletic training at all. Like any art or craft, however, the first step in learning preaching is to pay attention. Specifically, in a homiletic classroom, we attend to three things: the preacher's operative theology, methods for biblical and congregational interpretation, and rhetorical skills for proclamation and public speech. Ronald E Osborn, in *Folly of God: The Rise of Christian Preaching,* aptly describes these three ventures that together comprise the discipline of homiletics:

> The work of the preacher within the biblical tradition involves three kinds of tasks. *Exegesis* is the faithful discovery of the

---

[4] See the first national goal in the 1982 Appendix of *Fulfilled in Your Hearing,* 43.

[5] Gregory Heille, OP, 'The State of Catholic Preaching: What's Happening in the Pulpits of Our Parishes on Sunday and Is It What We Really Want?', *Seminary Journal* 5: 3 (Winter 1999), 38-39.

original intention of the text. As soon as the preacher moves to the situation of the hearers, *theology* comes to the fore; it is critical reflection on the faith received through the tradition in the effort to relate it to contemporary categories of thought. (Theologizing about the process of moving from text to application is called 'hermeneutic'). *Rhetoric* is the art of formulating the message so derived and delivering it in persuasive address. Together these three ventures constitute the discipline of homiletics, the art of making a sermon.[6]

The first three courses of the Aquinas Institute Doctor of Ministry in Preaching curriculum—Theology of Preaching, Biblical Hermeneutics and Preaching, and the Core Homiletic Seminar—attend to these three tasks in turn, in each area seeking insight, integration, and transformation of the preacher.

Differing theologies

The operative assumption behind this book is 'Differing Theologies: Differing Expectations for Preaching'.[7]

In Catholic thinking, there is a tradition that preaching is the 'first theology' and dogmatic or systematic theology (academic theology) is the 'second theology', the purpose of the second being to serve the first. Preaching, as theological reflection, is the summit and source of the ministry of the Word as it brings the Gospel to life in the catechesis, paraclesis, and evangelization of culture in a local Christian community. Preaching, when well served by theology, can be a naming of the grace at work in the community, even as it is a call to action for Christian discipleship in a sinful and broken world.

It makes sense, therefore, for preachers to engage in ongoing, critical study of (second) theology—in light of their experience as preaching (first) theologians in local communities of faith. This demanding process involves three steps: (1) re-examining the historical tradition with respect to a particular question or dogma, (2) critically naming and probing the questions and difficulties one faces when bringing this traditional understanding into dialogue with one's context of Christian life and ministry, and (3) re-articulating one's theological understanding in as meaningful a way as possible.

This three-step, historical-critical method of constructing or reconstructing theology can be understood in the expression of Hans Küng

---

[6] Ronald E Osborn, *Folly of God: The Rise of Christian Preaching* (St Louis: Chalice, 1997), 145.

[7] David Greenhaw, 'Theology of Preaching', in *Concise Encyclopedia of Preaching*, ed. William H Willimon and Richard Lischer (Louisville: Westminster John Knox, 1995), 479.

as *fides quaerens intellectum historicum* ('faith seeking historical understanding') or as 'critical ecumenical theology'—'a theology that is free and true, that knows its obligation to the scholarly ethos of truth, to methodological discipline, and the Church's supervision of the way it poses all the issues, of its methods, and results'[8] and 'a theology that sees in every other theology not an opponent but a partner, is bent on understanding instead of separation. ... And this is entirely meant to serve the *mission* of the Church in this society.'[9] Küng assumes, 'Only the theology that takes into consideration the problems posed by history itself, and answers them to the limit of its ability, is a theology equal to the demands of a contemporary awareness of the problems ... and is in this sense a scholarly theology that is truly up to date.'[10]

In the following essays, you will find numerous references to the work of Douglas John Hall, a theologian of the United Church of Canada, recently retired from McGill University, Montreal. Regrettably, this outstanding North American systematic theologian is little known in Catholic circles, even though his work is one of the finest examples of the historical-critical reconstruction of theology.

Hall has written a three-volume contextual Christian theology for North America.[11] In the first volume, *Thinking the Faith,* Hall reflects at length on how to do theological reflection, not 'in the abstract but concretely within a quite specific time and place'.[12] The second volume, *Professing the Faith*, critically reconstructs a theological understanding in the North American context of God (theology) creaturely being (anthropology), and Christ (christology). In Hall's description,

> While the first book asks *how* we think as Christians, the second asks *what* we think; that is, what is the *focus* of our thinking, its *meditative core*, so to speak? What in particular do Christians think *about?* What is the fundamental credo that we profess? ...
> ... Again, however, it is not my intention merely to present *the tradition*, but I shall attempt to bring it into dialogue with the secular and religious assumptions dominant in our

---

8   Hans Küng, *Theology for the Third Millennium* (New York: Doubleday, 1988), 161.

9   *Ibid.*, 162.

10   *Ibid.*, 112.

11   Douglas John Hall, *Thinking the Faith* (Minneapolis: Fortress, 1991), *Professing the Faith* (1993), *Confessing the Faith* (1996). Another fine work of Hall is *God and Human Suffering: An Exercise in the Theology of the Cross* (1986).

12   Hall, *Thinking the Faith*, 53.

culture, as I am able to discern them. ... [Otherwise,] we shall not be 'doing theology', but only reciting doctrine.[13]

The third volume, *Confessing the Faith*, demonstrates an implicit bridge between theology and ethics in a study of the Church (ecclesiology) and the Reign of God (eschatology), as well as 'the relation between church and world, the mission of the church, the meaning of ministry, worship, sacraments, and, above all, the character of Christian hope'.[14] Hall writes:

> Expressed in its most direct form, the calling of the Christian community is to *confess* the faith. That is, the church is summoned, always, to discover and announce for its time and place what it believes to be 'gospel'. It will not be *gospel* if the church simply recites its accumulated dogma, whether in the form of scripture and exegesis, historic creeds and confessions, liturgies, or systems of theology. It will be *gospel* only if it is *the right word, the right deed*—namely, what is *then and there* appropriate.[15]

The authors of the following essays all have read Hall's second volume, *Professing the Faith*, in which Hall applies historical-critical method in a North American context to reconstruct a Christian understanding of God, the human person, and Jesus Christ. Hall addresses each of these three dimensions of theological enquiry with three extensive chapters of historical theology, critical theology, and constructive theology. In theological shorthand, this methodology is one of *see-judge-act*.

As the preachers in this volume evaluate the Christian theological tradition in the light of their pastoral experience, there are, as you will see, pressing issues of concern in constructing a meaningful theology for contemporary preaching. Perhaps the most pressing question with respect to our understanding of God is that of the viability for today of a *theology of glory* (using Hall's term). Since Constantine and the birth of Christendom, 'The Christian doctrine of God has tended to accentuate the aspects of transcendence and power, as befits a patriarchally conceived deity in the service of empire.'[16] But how closely do we now want to associate Christ with empire, after a century that associates empire with the Second World War, the Cold War, the Cultural Revolution, Vietnam, and now low intensity wars of siege and attrition against civilians and indigenous peoples? Can a

---

[13] *Ibid.*, 54.
[14] *Ibid.*
[15] *Ibid.*, 55.
[16] Hall, *Professing the Faith*, 92.

God of glory be in solidarity with the displaced, the bereaved, and the poor?

Hall reconstructs God as a god who suffers. As much as this proposal appeals to many preachers, this solution always seems to me to be an anthropomorphism and not quite a solution. Certainly, if we are to keep faith with the dead and the dispossessed, our preaching must question the so-called God of glory. But if not glory, then what?

Contemporary faith must struggle equally with the scandal of a high or glorious anthropology. Human beings, after all, have done the violence that shakes our faith in a god of empire and glory. Enlightenment faith in the myth of progress hardly speaks to the actuality of billions of displaced and struggling people. We humans believe we are made in the image and likeness of God, but what does this mean if we can no longer march to the anthem of cross and crown, Christendom and empire? In what does human dignity consist for displaced and powerless people?

Perhaps at no place other than the foot of the cross do all our questions about God's divinity and our humanity become so essential. Hall writes:

> What Paul means when he asserts that he is determined to know and to preach only the one thing, 'Jesus Christ, and him crucified,' is that for him this represents the foundation and core of the whole Christian profession of belief. That is to say, he intends to consider every subject from the perspective that one acquires upon it when it is considered from the vantage point of the cross.[17]

What meaning does our Christian expression, 'God sacrificed his only son', give to the memory of Jewish children sacrificed in the crematoria of Auschwitz and Dachau or Muslim children dying as a consequence of sanctions in Iraq or Christian children dying of AIDS in Africa? Just how does Jesus helpfully represent God to the pathos of our world, and how does Jesus restore our dignity with God? How does Jesus save, and how are we to talk about him from the pulpit?

Differing expectations of preaching

The following essays also make frequent reference to Mary Catherine Hilkert and her use of the expressions *dialectical imagination* and *sacramental imagination*. A Dominican sister from Akron, Ohio, Professor Hilkert teaches in the

---

[17] *Ibid.*, 363-64.

department of theology at the University of Notre Dame, in Indiana. In 1988, while on the faculty of Aquinas Institute of Theology, Hilkert published a classic article in the Catholic theology of preaching: 'Naming Grace: A Theology of Proclamation'.[18] Over the following years of teaching the Theology of Preaching course in the Doctor of Ministry in Preaching program at Aquinas Institute, and after publication of several additional articles, Professor Hilkert gathered her work into a groundbreaking volume for Catholic homiletics: *Naming Grace: Preaching and the Sacramental Imagination*.[19] In this volume, Hilkert struggles with the sorts of questions that have been raised here about our contemporary understanding of God, the human person, and Jesus Christ, and how these understandings translate meaningfully into the language of the pulpit.

The first chapters of *Naming Grace* are titled 'The Dialectical Imagination: The Power of the Word', 'The Sacramental Imagination: Grace Enfleshed in Word and Action', and 'Preaching as the Art of Naming Grace'. Hilkert uses the image of a diptych of two icons to convey the recent situation in systematic theology—the dialectical icon representing the theology of Karl Barth and Rudolf Bultmann and the sacramental icon representing the theology of Karl Rahner and Edward Schillebeeckx, with the hinge that joins the two icons representing the theology of Paul Tillich. This entire theological diptych is a window of insight onto the world of contemporary preaching.

Franz Kafka once remarked that words are like an ice axe. In the context of the rise of National Socialism in Germany, during which all five of these theologians were contemporaries, Karl Barth took up the ice axe of God's Word. Barth (1886-1968) and his Protestant contemporaries in the seminary had been raised in the Protestant Enlightenment tradition in which the father of Protestant liberalism, Friedrich Schleiermacher (1768-1834), argued in *Speeches on Religion for Its Cultured Despisers* that, by finding God in the wonders of human experience, a Christian can aspire to be simultaneously a modern and a believer. However, contemplating his experience as a Reformed pastor in Switzerland, Barth felt bound in conscience to say that the image of God in an exalted humanity had been radically severed by sin, that enlightened efforts to find God by human efforts were misguided and futile, and that the preacher's task was to announce God's Word in Scripture as a transcendent force breaking in upon and smashing through human experience, like an ice axe. This is an example of the *dialectical imagination*.

---

[18] Mary Catherine Hilkert, 'Naming Grace: A Theology of Proclamation', *Worship* 60 (September 1986): 434-49.

[19] Mary Catherine Hilkert, *Naming Grace: Preaching and the Sacramental Imagination* (New York, Continuum, 1997).

A helpful question for understanding the dialectical imagination is to ask about the point of contact between the Word of God and human experience. Barth said there is no point of contact. God is utterly outside our sinful and evil human experience and therefore in dialectical relationship to it. Rudolf Bultmann (1884-1976), a Lutheran pastor in Germany, shared Barth's dialectical emphasis on the wholly-other God and on sinful human experience. However, he differed from Barth by saying we do have a point of contact in our human experience for receiving the Word of God—the existential dilemma of our sinfulness.

Paul Tillich (1886-1965), another German Lutheran who did much of his theology in the United States of America, answered the point-of-contact question by saying that revelation is the answer to the question of human existence which rises up from within our experience. Tillich introduced the theological idea of *correlation*—a theological conversation between the scriptural tradition and history and human experience—as the locus for revelation. This idea of correlation honors both the dialectical imagination (by saying that the point of contact is a question which points to an answer in the still-transcendent God) and the sacramental imagination (by raising up human experience as a partner in the theological conversation).

The theological context for the Jesuit theologian Karl Rahner (1904-1984) was different in one aspect. In addition to being profoundly affected by the Nazi occupation of Austria, Rahner also was coming to theological terms with his seminary training in neo-scholasticism.[20] As Rahner worked to retrieve from neo-scholasticism the Thomistic understanding of grace building upon nature, he posited a world in which the image of God in the human person and in human experience is not fundamentally obliterated by sin. Creation, history, and experience provide a continuing point of contact for the revelation of God's grace. As a consequence, with *sacramental imagination* (David Tracy's phrase is *analogical imagination*), the preacher's task and the task of the believing community is to name the grace of God in experience: hence, Mary Catherine Hilkert's expression, *naming grace*.

But with this accent on grace, what about sin? A Belgian Dominican, Edward Schillebeeckx (1914-), grappled with this critical question which the dialectical imagination asks of the sacramental imagination throughout a distinguished theological career which led, in the 1970s and 80s, to a meditation on human experience in its negativity and on radical suffering in its meaninglessness and senselessness—to which Schillebeeckx gave the name, *contrast experience.*

---

[20] See Thomas F O'Meara, *Thomas Aquinas: Theologian* (Notre Dame, IN/London, UK: University of Notre Dame, 1997), for a clear treatment of neo-scholasticism.

Later chapters of *Naming Grace* grapple at length with the question as to whether grace can be named in the contrast experience of radical suffering and evil. In our post-Holocaust world, Karl Barth's critique of religious naiveté must neither be forgotten nor taken lightly. Those of us who cherish the sacramental imagination and who instinctively preach by naming the grace of creation and of human experience must learn also to name disgrace and at times raise the axe of a more dialectical and transcendent Word.

Wherever we may place ourselves on the dialectical-sacramental spectrum, the Word of God proves to be bigger than our theological predispositions. Contemplation of the dialectical-sacramental diptych forces preachers to take the Word of God more seriously. The challenge is not to choose between oversimplified Protestant and Catholic or dialectical and sacramental understandings of preaching. The challenge is to engage in a more nuanced dialogue that illuminates and honors the preaching act.[21]

The authors of the following essays give their primary loyalty, without exception, to the sacramental imagination. As they struggle with difficulty to understand the dialectical-sacramental distinction, however, their sacramental loyalties to naming and preaching the grace of God, present in creation and in the unfolding history of human experience, must come to terms with the harsh critique of the post-Holocaust and postmodern search for meaning. At risk is the theological plausibility of their preaching.

Differing preachers

My father, Ed Heille, was a high school mathematics teacher who firmly believed that students in his classroom were studying him as a person—his character—more than geometry or trigonometry. So, too, with preaching: the preacher, in his or her person, is a message. In the rhetorical disciplines, the word for this connection of person to message is *ēthos* (pronounced as a long *a*). André Resner, an authority on *ēthos* in preaching, writes: '*Ēthos* has to do with the nature of character and virtue in the speaker.'[22]

Not only must a preacher articulate a plausible operative theology, anthropology, and christology and develop a nuanced understanding of what

---

[21] Hilkert, 195: 'For a helpful overview of the distinction between the dialectical imagination and the analogical imagination, see David Tracy, *The Analogical Imagination: Christian Theology in a Culture of Pluralism* (New York: Crossroad, 1981), 405-45. Sallie McFague makes a similar point in terms of Protestant and Catholic "sensibilities". See *Metaphorical Theology: Models of God in Religious Language* (Philadelphia: Fortress, 1982) 13-14.'

[22] André Resner Jr, *Preacher and Cross: Person and Message in Theology and Rhetoric* (Grand Rapids, MI/Cambridge, UK: William B Eerdmans, 1999), 19.

is at stake in the dialectical and sacramental imagination. If the preacher wishes to reach the goal of the preaching vocation, which is *to confess the faith* (to use Hall's expression), the preacher must also tend to the spiritual life and the life of virtue, to his her Christian character.

This is in part a matter of tending to one's rhetorical integrity: Does your *ēthos* as a speaker confess or witness to the faith which you theologically profess? Does your rhetoric reveal or mask your character? When your people study you, are they learning what you want them to learn about God, about themselves, about Jesus Christ? When people are scandalized by you, is the scandal authentically Christian, or are you—at the level of character—a cause of false scandal?

One of the most helpful aids I have found for enabling experienced students of preaching to reflect on their character as preachers is a set of strategic planning exercises for the preaching ministry. We begin by reading the first part of Joseph M Webb's, *Preaching and the Challenge of Pluralism*. In this book, Webb steps out from theology into a sociological consideration of preaching by reviewing groundbreaking research into conflict and diversity by the sociologists of the University of Chicago early in the last century. The Chicago theory concludes that we act in different ways and enter into conflict together because of emotionally freighted *hub symbols*:

> These are the symbols that are invested by their holder with so much emotional charge that they become the "ultimate" symbols to that person. They are invested with full personal and collective sanctity, at least for the person who holds them at the center. Moreover, they are sacred in the sense that they *must not* and *cannot* be derogated by someone else without their holder's feeling violated in some ultimate sense.[23]

With Webb's remarks on 'symbolic autobiography'[24] as their guide, I ask preaching students to write a *values statement*, identifying the hub symbols and the origin of these core values in the story of their lives. This is the first step in a process of journal entries by which each student sets out to make the following articulations, in the general format of a strategic plan for the preaching ministry.[25]

---

[23] Joseph M Webb, *Preaching and the Challenge of Pluralism* (St Louis: Chalice, 1998), 50.

[24] *Ibid.*, 58-59.

[25] I thank Carmelita Murphy, OP, of LEAD, Inc., Grand Rapids, MI, for much of what I have learned about strategic planning. See also Ray Kesner, 'Vocational Discernment' in *Experiencing Ministry Supervision: A Field-Based Approach*, ed. William T Pyle and Mary Alice Seals (Nashville: Broadman and Holman, 1995), 33-48.

In a *vision statement*, the preachers are first asked to dream dreams and to write about their vision of the preaching ministry for the Church.

In the *call* or *vocation statement* preachers are asked to say why they are in the preaching ministry, how they are gifted for preaching, and the ministerial roles toward which they are moving as preachers.[26] The preachers consider their 'fundamental call to salvation, holiness, and intimate relationship with God'[27], as well as their sense of being set apart by God for some particular ministry. How has life—with its gifts, abilities, muddles, and struggles[28]—pointed the preacher vocationally on his or her way? Furthermore, how has the preacher received an ecclesiastical call from his or her congregation or denomination?

Vocational identity as preachers 'demands that what we are about in our ministries be congruent with the things to which we attach the highest value. To the extent that values and vocational demands are out of sync, to that degree our sense of integrity is called into question and self-worth is diminished.'[29] In the *values statement*, the preachers are asked to return to their work with Webb and hub symbols and to restate their core values—in terms of their relationship to the vision and call statements.

'A *mission statement* is at the heart of intentional ministry.'[30] Citing Stephen Covey in *Seven Habits of Highly Effective People*, Ray Kesner writes, 'With a well-executed mission statement you are empowered with an instrument against which every "decision concerning the most effective use of your time, talents, and your energies" may be measured.'[31] As preachers write mission statements, they are advised also to mention any denominational or congregational mission statements in which they are stakeholders and to evaluate their sense of ownership or commitment to these mission statements.

Preachers are then asked to articulate *opportunities, threats, strengths, and weaknesses* in themselves, in their organizations, and in the culture, as these apply to their preaching vision, vocation, and mission. What, finally, are the most *critical issues* which, if they continue, will have a significant effect on arriving at the goal of the preaching vocation?

José Luis Quintana is one of twenty doctoral students in preaching, including the authors of the following essays, who recently completed these strategic planning exercises to examine his vocation and character as a preacher. After doing so, he sat down with an artist from his parish to make a visual

---

[26] *Cf.* Kesner, 36–37.

[27] *Ibid.*, 37.

[28] *Ibid.*, 37–38.

[29] *Ibid.*, 39.

[30] *Ibid.*

[31] Kesner, 38–39, citing Stephen R Covey, *The Seven Habits of Highly Effective People: Restoring the Character Ethic* (New York: Fireside, 1990), 108–09.

representation of himself as a preacher. The painting shows the complexity of one preacher's world—a Catholic from Durango, Mexico, who came as a young man to Mundelein Seminary in Chicago and was then ordained to serve for the Diocese of Grand Rapids, Michigan; a North American priest, and yet an alien in an alien land; a tender and caring pastor, holding in his hands pastoral responsibility to the diverse and changing congregation of his Grand Rapids parish, while maintaining numerous ties to the extended community of first, second, and third generation Hispanic Catholics of West Michigan.

In his call statement, José writes that he feels like the prophet Amos: 'I was not a preacher, nor am I a son of a preacher; I was a shepherd. The Lord took me from following the flock and said to me, "Go, preach and comfort my people in an alien land."'[32] His mission statement is a window into the changing and pluralistic world of contemporary preaching. It is all the more remarkable because it is the mission statement of an 'American priest':

> I, José Quintana, a foreign preacher in a foreign land, am called by God and empowered by the Church to preach the word of the Living God in a multicultural world. I am impelled to commit my life and time to the preparation and proclamation of the Gospel in solidarity with the poor in a foreign land. I am a preacher on a journey. I struggle to preach and live out Gospel values in a foreign land, in a foreign language, and in a foreign culture. I am summoned to preach and to live the cross of Christ. I am called not only to preach eloquently the matters of Christ's cross, but also to embody in my existence the mystery of the cross. I am called to bear the gospel values in what I say and do.
>
> My commitment to this ministry impels me to serve as a bridge among the cultures. I am called to demonstrate how it is possible to cross cultural boundaries and to enter into the world of the other culture. If I wait long enough and listen hard enough, I will gain the capacity to understand new voices, voices that create new hope and new understanding of different cultures.
>
> I recognize that preaching is a privilege and a great responsibility. I gratefully exercise it with God's grace.[33]

---

[32] *Cf.* Amos 7: 14–15.
[33] Quoted with permission of the author.

In the essays that follow, you are invited into the diverse theological and pastoral worlds of eight dedicated preachers, seven Catholics and an Episcopalian—a deacon recently retired from university teaching in London, a priest beginning her ministry in West Missouri, a Nigerian priest studying in the United States, another priest in campus ministry at Iowa State University, a concert vocalist in Indiana pursuing a lay ecclesial vocation to pastoral ministry, an itinerant Redemptorist preacher from the Bronx, a diocesan pastor and vocation director from Pennsylvania, and a rural Catholic pastor and chaplain for a children's home in North Dakota.

The essays have been ordered somewhat intuitively but can be read in any order. They are given with gratitude to the wisdom community of Christian preachers, with a prayer that Christian preaching be engaged with imagination and integrity in our word-saturated and God-hungry world.

GOD SO LOVED THE WORLD
Duncan Macpherson

The renewal of the theology of the Trinity lies at the heart of all Christian renewal, including the theology of preaching. Expressive of an inexpressible reality, the doctrine of the Trinity structures the preaching message. It is the framework of the Christian experience and the foundation of Christian praxis. The renewal of the theology of the Trinity is also important for the dialogue with other faiths, as well as with atheism. Christian anthropology sees Christ as the goal of evolution, with humanity as essentially communitarian, created for communion with God and with others. In this, humanity mirrors, to some degree, the social reality of the Trinity. Collectively flawed by sin, humanity finds a new solidarity in Christ. The preaching of this message should have consequences that are both personal and political.

The vision, call, and mission of the preacher

The vision of the preacher must be primarily one of faithful discipleship, and discipleship involves finding a share in the preaching task of the Church. This task is not limited to bringing the Christian message to unbelievers. It embraces the whole task of evangelisation—the bringing of the good news to the world. It is good news for the poor, involving work for justice and peace, the 'breaking of unjust fetters'. It is the good news in catechesis for adults, as well as for the young. It is proclaimed not only by word, but also by the witness of loving communion among Christians, as well as by unselfish service of the wider human family. In the context of the liturgy, preaching involves aspects of all these facets of the ministry of the Word. In addition to developing the spiritual and theological understanding of committed members of the Body of Christ, preaching often involves the proclamation of good news to those who are Christian only in name. To be authentic it must also address social and political issues, contribute to Christian formation and theological education, foster community within the Church, and promote an active commitment to service.

The homily always should involve the rehearsal of the saving events of the incarnation, death, and resurrection of Christ in a way that invites the listeners to repentance and a deeper commitment of faith, hope, and love. This rehearsal draws upon both a dialectical and a sacramental imagination,[1] the dialectical imagination emphasising God's transcendence and human sinfulness,[2] and the sacramental imagination stressing God's reign as already present, through grace, within human experience. In the light of this writer's Catholic identity and formative theological influences, this essay is more disposed to the sacramental hermeneutic than to the dialectical. Moreover, modern catechetical theory has shown the importance of connecting with life experience.[3] Still, these two tendencies are not determined purely by denominational identity or theological school. Pastoral context often directs the approach taken. Most importantly in preaching, the biblical text itself may invite one or another emphasis. Some texts emphasise the transcendent holiness of God in relation to the sinfulness of human beings; others invite reflection upon the manifestations by which God is already present, working in the hearts of men and women, even if this presence is not yet recognised. A dialectical message emphasises the judgment implicit in the love and generosity of God and asks: Where am I, the hearer, in the face of such generosity; what needs to be changed in me, and in the world, loved so much by God that he gave his only begotten Son? The sacramental or analogical message emphasises the way in which God's love is already present in the hearts and experience of the hearers, waiting to be recognized and named, under the influence of the Holy Spirit—without forgetting the negative experiences and suffering of these same hearers. 'The preacher represents this community by voicing its concerns, naming its demons, thus enabling it to gain some ownership and control of the evil that afflicts it.'[4] This

---

[1] Mary Catherine Hilkert, *Naming Grace: Preaching and the Sacramental Imagination* (New York: Continuum, 1997), 19-43.

[2] Barth's understanding of the dialectic owed more to Kierkegaard and Dostoievsky than to Hegel and centres on the idea that God's revelation can only be affirmed by the recognition that the one who receives it is not the 'new man'. There are, however, different understandings of dialectical theology in Bultmann and others, based on the dialectic of Heidegger and Buber. Tillich, too, finds some place for analogical imagination within his dialectical tradition (Hilkert, 27-29).

[3] Catechetical writers making this emphasis include Johannes Hofinger in the late 1950s, Gabriel Moran in the 1960s, and Thomas Groome in the 1980s.

[4] Bishops' Committee on Priestly Life and Ministry, National Conference of Catholic Bishops, *Fulfilled in Your Hearing: The Homily in the Sunday Assembly* (Washington, DC: United States Catholic Conference, 1982), 7-8.

representation is what Edward Schillebeeckx sees as the way in which God is present in 'the pain of contrast', holding out hope where it is least anticipated, as 'unexpected grace'.[5] Which of these emphases is operative in the outlook of any one preacher is often affected by the social context prevailing in a particular place and time.[6]

A preacher's values should be formed by the gospel message itself, by the tradition of interpretation of that message in the context of the experience of the believing community, and also by dialogue with the cultural milieu in which the Gospel is preached. Whatever the core values of the Christian preacher, a clear understanding of the incarnation should avoid 'both the Scylla of conservative exclusivity and the Charybdis of liberal generalities'.[7] These include *fundamentalism* (including Catholic fundamentalism) on the one hand and *perspectivism* on the other. The incarnational approach has a concern for the objective reality of the content of revelation, but it differs from fundamentalism because it recognises that all truths are mediated through historical and sociological relativities. Perspectivism is a term that covers reductive postmodern forms of pluralistic theological liberalism. In the confused period of late capitalism in which we live, everything appears as a commodity that can be bought, according to the individual consumer's preference. Perspectivism respects both pluralism and personal choice, but it introduces an inverse fundamentalism of political correctness, in which nobody may say that one person's beliefs or values are more or less correct than anybody else's. It is small wonder that fundamentalism is flourishing. By so weakening the healthy capacity for critique, characteristic of post-Enlightenment modernism, perspectivism encourages confused and frightened people to take refuge in certainties that they are no longer expected to justify. Perspectivism itself offers the comparable certainties of 'inverse fundamentalism'.[8]

The preacher is primarily a human being, committed to trying to fulfil the call to a fuller life, for him or herself, and for humanity. He or she is

---

[5] Hilkert, 15-53.

[6] See Gregory Baum, *The Twentieth Century: A Theological Overview* (New York, Orbis, 1999). Each of the contributions to this symposium focuses upon major events, disasters, and movements in the twentieth century and examines their impact upon Christian theology in one or more ecclesial communities in one or more geographical areas. The practical relevance of all this for the preacher derives from the close connection between theology (the understanding of the message in a changing cultural context) and homiletics (the communication of the Gospel in the light of that understanding).

[7] Douglas John Hall, *Professing the Faith: Christian Theology in a North American Context* (Minneapolis: Fortress, 1993), 15.

[8] I am indebted to my friend and former colleague Jim Byrne, currently Associate Professor at Saint Michael's College, Colchester, Vermont, for this understanding and use of the term *perspectivism*.

called to affirm and to further everything that sets human beings free to fulfil their potential as children of God and to oppose whatever limits or undermines it. This involves a particular commitment to working for justice and peace. As a Christian, the preacher will be committed to identifying ways in which Christian discipleship can strengthen, deepen, and enrich the human project, as well as to find ways in which Christianity can help in its successful advancement. Those whose discipleship is part of the discipleship of the Catholic Church will be committed to serving the Church, promoting its mission, engaging in fellowship and renewal, respecting its teachings, working for the wider unity of Christians, and seeking understanding between peoples of all faiths and none. In turn, these commitments require that the preacher should promote them through study, prayer, and being available to the needs of others.

Christian preaching involves the communication of the good news of God's self-disclosure in the person of Jesus Christ and inviting men and women to enter into fuller communion, both with God and with each other, through the gift of the Holy Spirit. This message offers reassurance, but it also challenges sin and injustice at both the personal and the societal level. If this message of reassurance and challenge is to be received, it needs to be incarnated clearly and powerfully within the experience and the language of those for whom it is intended. Whether it is imparted with a more or less dialectical or sacramental-analogical emphasis will depend on the text and context of the message. The preacher's understanding is informed both by lived experience and by theological understanding. Key preaching strengths consist in the ability to identify the core message of the appointed scripture readings and the skill to communicate this message in ways appropriate to a particular congregation.

Threats to the success of the preacher are both external and internal. Secularism and indifference to faith outside the Church represent the main external threat, whereas the failure of those inside the Church to appreciate the importance of good preaching can also represent a serious obstacle. For Catholics, the general limitation of preaching at Mass to ordained men critically limits the pool of good preachers available for this essential ministry.[9]

Other primary critical issues for preaching centre on the personal faith and character of the preacher (André Resner's *ēthos*[10]), which is fundamental to the credibility of the message. However, the opportunities presented by a preaching ministry are only the means to an end. That end is

---

[9] Hilkert, 144–94.

[10] André Resner Jr, *Preacher and Cross: Person and Message in Theology and Rhetoric* (Grand Rapids, MI/Cambridge, UK: William B Eerdmans, 1999).

one of loving service in response to God's call. The one who is called does not depend upon his or her strengths and should not be put off by weaknesses or even failure. Opportunities should be used, and threats blocked, according to what is practicable, but the only really critical issue is one of faithful discipleship.

A trinitarian theology of preaching

My theology of Christian preaching is a theology of the Holy Trinity—centred on christological understanding and expressive of a dynamic Christian anthropology. Because understanding develops within the framework of history, a theology of the Trinity must be historical and critical. As the core doctrine of Christian faith, it must also be ecumenical—both in relation to other Christian identities and also to those of other religious and non-religious convictions.[11]

The only area of Christian theology that can be treated separately from the Trinity is natural theology, the discussion of the divine within a philosophical framework that does not presuppose faith.[12] The Trinity is the framework and the heart of both revealed theology and Christian experience. It is the way in which God is known by those who have been changed through their encounter with Jesus Christ. The first followers of Jesus already had a faith firmly based on the absolute oneness of God. However they found that there were things they felt obliged to say about Jesus that, hitherto, they could only say about God himself. The divine was now experienced through Jesus as brother, conferring a 'Spirit of adoption', enabling human beings to become sons and daughters of the Father and brothers and sisters to each other.

Central to Christian preaching, the Trinity is never just one doctrine among others. It expresses, in human terms, an inexpressible reality, utterly beyond imagination and the scope of ordinary human thinking, a paradoxical truth expressed only falteringly through the language of negation and analogy. A fuller account of the doctrine of the Trinity would provide a historical and critical account of the process by which the disciples were compelled to revise some of their beliefs in the light of their experience, making constructive use of images used in the Old Testament to describe the attributes and actions of God. The application of these images contributed to fierce debate

---

[11] Hans Küng, *Theology for the Third Millennium* (New York: Doubleday, 1988).
[12] Dialectical theology excludes the possibility of natural theology because it denies the legitimate use of the language of analogy. For example, see Hall, 44–51.

in the later history of the early Church, and it is out of the heat of these controversies, with all their very human political ramifications, that the classical Christian formulations of the doctrine of the Trinity emerged.[13] These formulations remain authentic and necessary for the faith of the Church, defining ('setting limits to') and providing the structure for the way Christians talk about the Trinity. This structure needs to be recovered as the basis for Church renewal—in preaching, catechesis, liturgy, and prayer, as well as in renewed commitment to revering the human person and transforming the modern world.

The experience of God through Christ changes the lives of believers, placing them in a new relationship with God and each other. This changed relationship is described simultaneously in three distinct and interrelated ways.[14] Jesus is experienced as God. Placing himself alongside humanity in his living and dying, Jesus opens up a new relationship with the God to whom he prayed: the God he called Father. Through the relationship with Jesus as brother, the Christian experiences God revealed in familiar and intimate terms as being like a loving, instantly accessible parent. The reality that forms the galaxies of stars and rules the destiny of nations can now be called *Abba*, or Father. Finally, through the action and prayer of Jesus, his brothers and sisters experience the generosity of the Father. This generosity is manifested as the gift of the Holy Spirit who is active as a new transforming power in their lives. The same power that raised Jesus from the dead is now the gift of God breaking down barriers of misunderstanding and estrangement, assuring men and women of their status as brothers and sisters of Jesus and therefore as children of God as Father. In each of these three distinct experiences of God Christians still perceive an essential oneness of transcendent being, differing only in the relations, as and between, the three persons of Father, Son, and Holy Spirit.

It is obvious that these definitions sometimes seem remote, reflecting historical controversies, without clear relevance to today. However the experience and the decisions of past generations of Christians remain an important safeguard against error as new theologies reflect the faith within

---

[13] The word *Trinity* (Greek *Trias*) is first used by Theophilus of Antioch around 180, but the doctrine only received its authoritative formulations at the Council of Nicaea, 325, and Constantinople, 381. Together these formulations were drawn up to exclude Arianism, which denied the full divinity of the Son, and Macedonianism, which denied the full divinity of the Holy Spirit.

[14] Hall rightly stresses this emphasis on the Trinity as relational, but he is not justified in inferring from this that substantialist notions about the Trinity are to be excluded. God is what God does. Hall's neo-orthodoxy, on the other hand, precludes our saying what God is, just as it excludes the frank acknowledgement that Jesus is God (165).

new worlds of language and ideas.

However, the Trinity remains fundamental to our attempts to close the gap between theology and life. Liberation theology offers the insight that theology is not something that is talked about, but something to be done— *theoretical action*. Effective trinitarian renewal needs to be both intellectually rigorous and devotionally alive, rooted equally in prayer and action. Direct prayer to Jesus or to the Holy Spirit can never be excluded. However, the classical model of prayer to the Father through the Son and in the Spirit should be the fundamental principal and norm for both private and communal prayer. Such an approach issues directly into fresh strategies, both for preaching and for political and social action. Although this formulation is akin to Marx's idea of praxis (or practical theory),[15] its roots lie in Jesus' New Testament teaching.[16] Hence, a renewal in the theology of the Trinity will not just rehearse the themes of Scripture and the church fathers, reinterpreting them within the framework of modern and postmodern systems of thought. Such an enterprise could easily degenerate into a clever game with words. Theology, spirituality, preaching, and social and political action must all be renewed by rediscovering the dynamics of how the Father continues to express his love in and through the risen Jesus, breathing his Spirit into a new redeemed humanity.[17]

Renewal in trinitarian understanding is vital for renewal in all areas of Christian faith and life. In the period preceding the start of the Second Vatican Council in 1961, the Roman Catholic pioneers of liturgical and catechetical renewal drew attention to the continuing and paradoxical consequence of the fight against Arianism centuries before. Excluding any suggestion that Jesus as God was in any way inferior to God the Father, the divinity of Christ had been emphasised in such a way as to eclipse his role as the mediator between human beings and the Father.

More recently, movement toward dialogue with other world religions has sometimes led to a tendency to question the universal truth claims of Christianity. This has led to a relativist perception of the doctrine of the Trinity. Those who are part of this interfaith movement often feel uncomfortable with the apparently exclusive perspective of the trinitarian vision. Viewed superficially, the saying of Jesus, 'No one comes to the Father except through me,'[18] seems to constitute too exclusivist an account of the spiritual and ethical experience of humanity.

---

[15] Baum offers a clear statement of the concept in an otherwise confused contribution on 'The Impact of Marxist Ideas on Christian Theology' (182).

[16] See Matt. 8: 21-24 and 1 John 4: 19.

[17] John 20: 19-23.

[18] John 14: 6b *NRSV.*

Although these anti-trinitarian currents have had some influence in Roman Catholic theological circles, there have been factors in the renewal of Catholic theology that have mitigated their effects. Thus, the insights of the critical study of the Scriptures have been balanced by revivals in the classical systems of theology from the early church fathers to Thomism. So, too, in the encounter with other faiths the Catholic intellectual tradition has been better placed to develop an inclusivist approach that leaves the integrity of orthodox Christian theology unimpaired. Here, dialogue implies respect for the integrity of the partner in dialogue and co-operation in building a new community of love. An inclusivist approach also suggests that Christian understanding may be enriched by the insights of other faiths.

In the task of proclaiming the good news to unbelievers, Christians clearly have been in difficulty for some time. Secular post-Christian thinking seems unable to form any clear idea of what is meant by God. God may indeed have 'so loved the world,'[19] but if no clear meaning can be attached to the subject of the sentence, it remains an unsigned love letter, leaving the recipient rather cold. At the intellectual level Marx, Freud, Sartre, and Russell have all done an effective job on demolishing the idea of God. Meanwhile, at the popular level, belief in God is often no more than a residual notion of a 'spirit in the sky'. To get through to these contemporary mentalities it is necessary to rebuild the trinitarian character of the gospel message on what is sometimes referred to as a 'Christology from below'.[20] 'Christology from below' means starting from the concrete reality of the Jesus of the Gospels in all his human poverty and vulnerability. Although the Gospels are not biography in the modern sense, they are still reliable enough to confront us with a man who is capable of astounding the reader by his words and actions and of attracting total loyalty by the grace and power of his personality. Most significantly the reality experienced in the meeting with Jesus is identified as the one he calls Father. For the conscientious modern secular man or woman, an open-minded examination of the Jesus of the Gospels has the capacity to 're-open the file' on God. The next stage involves faith in the death of Jesus as the decisive expression of his total openness to the Father and in the resurrection of Jesus as the offer of new life in the Holy Spirit to those who believe. The validating experience here is not simply the subjective inner experience of the new believer, but also the experience of a radical change in the whole anthropological reality.

Christian anthropology is christological and, therefore, trinitarian. Just as Adam is a proto-typical figure of all human beings in their origin,

---

[19] John 3: 16 *NRSV.*
[20] Jon Sobrino, *Jesus the Liberator* (London: Burns Oates, 1994).

Christ represents humanity in its goal. In the Christian tradition the human person is a creature, a centre of consciousness, made in the image of God, intended for communion with God—the Supreme Consciousness—with and through other persons. As creature, the human person has solidarity with other creatures and with the whole of creation and is the product of an evolutionary process in which creatures reach progressively greater levels of complexity and consciousness. The human creature has evolved a capacity, not only to know, but also to be aware of knowing, with a capacity to determine, for good or ill, the future evolution, not only of humanity, but also of other creatures and of much of the rest of creation.[21]

In the understanding of scientist and theologian Teilhard de Chardin,[22] this provides a teleological perspective on the whole of evolution, with its goal in the incarnation of Christ. The incarnation marks the union of human and divine nature—the created and the uncreated consciousness. The present stage of evolution consists of what Teilhard calls christification—the coming together of the whole created order into oneness with God through human nature united with the divine nature in Christ. Although Teilhard has been criticised for producing a theology that is more poetic than analytic, it should be remembered that his work was forbidden publication by the church authorities of his time and was never honed by the criticism and comments of his peers. Nevertheless, his approach seems essential to the working out of any credible post-Darwinian Christian anthropology—not least for its christological emphasis.

This approach to Christian anthropology is also trinitarian. The Christ who is the mediator of the new creation is also the Word of the Father, the Word who is operative in creation, and the light of every human person coming into the world.[23] Augustine's image of the Trinity as analogous to the human personality with the threefold attributes of memory, will, and understanding implies that human beings, created in the image of God, mirror the Trinity in their own selfhood. His other analogy of God as Lover, Love, and Beloved suggests that communion is an essential aspect of the divine

---

[21] The concern with the environmental future is reflected in much modern theological writing. See, for example, Baum (219-28) and Hall (301-62). As with feminist theology, however, green theology always runs the risk of distracting us from the economic inequalities that represent the root cause contradiction which underlies the legitimate concerns of these theologies. The absence of class-based politics in the United States of America since the beginning of the Second World War and the defeat of the trades unions in the United Kingdom in the early 1980s might help to explain this phenomenon.

[22] *Le phénomène humain* (1955, Eng. tr. *The Phenomenon of Man*, 1959) and *Le milieu divin* (1957. Eng. tr. *The Divine Milieu*, 1960).

[23] John 1: 1-9.

nature and therefore crucial to any understanding of human nature. The human person, self-conscious consciousness, craves community with God and with others, mirroring the nature of the godhead. The frustration of this craving is attributed by Christianity to sin, literally 'missing the mark', although, as Douglas John Hall argues, the biblical understanding of sin suggests a much more decisive rejection of God's law.[24]

Since individual human beings share in frustration of community as part of their ontological and social experience, Christian theology posits original sin, making the myth of Adam and Eve's disobedience to God's command the symbolic framework for exploring the unfulfilled human potentiality to share more fully in the life of God and to relate more harmoniously with creation and with other human beings. Deprived of their intended God and other-centeredness, human persons experience a new solidarity in sin that expresses itself in social structures of alienation, violence, exploitation, and oppression. Jesus, who is of one substance not only with the Father but also with humanity, provides through his radical obedience to the Father a new kind of human solidarity based on openness to God and to others. This new solidarity, with its new system of values, is variously described in the Bible as 'the kingdom of God' in Mark and Luke, as 'the kingdom of heaven' in Matthew, as 'eternal life' in John, and as 'new creation' or 'the Body of Christ' in Paul.

This new solidarity is expressed explicitly in the sacramental life of the Church and in the spiritual life of each baptised person, but it is also present implicitly in what Paul Tillich calls 'ultimate concern', whereby human beings make a radical response to the reality of the kingdom, even where it is not named. This takes place in every initiative that re-centres human beings and breaks down the barriers to the fuller humanity for which they were created. Applied to social, economic, and political issues, it will stress the value of each human person, calling into question existing values, structures, and institutions in the name of something that, although it is already mysteriously present, will only be fully realised beyond history. Christian anthropology also has radical relevance for environmental concerns. Human solidarity with the rest of creation is based both on common creatureliness and upon communion with God through the cosmic, risen Christ. In some mysterious way, nature shares in the human predicament of suffering and incompleteness consequent upon sin and will share in some way in the ultimate victory. While this vision is still, in the best sense of the word, unashamedly anthropocentric, as well as christocentric, it takes seriously the responsibilities that humanity has towards nature if its own humanity is to flourish, or even to survive.

---

[24] Hall, 223.

The foregoing picture is intended to retain, and at some points to reinterpret, the essential elements of traditional Christian anthropology within a christological and trinitarian framework. As such, it does not find it necessary to include everything taught in earlier formulations, particularly those of Pope Pius the XII's encyclical *Humanae Generis*, published in 1950,[25] in which it is stressed that Adam and Eve represent real individuals from whom all human individuals are descended and through whom original sin has been transmitted. Many traditionalist Protestant and most Eastern Orthodox Christians probably share this interpretation in an even more literalistic form. It is interesting that Jews and Muslims do not derive any doctrine of original sin from their interpretation of the story of Adam. St Paul seems to have been the first person to develop this doctrine, and he does so in the light of his christology. Christians experience a new, collective coming alive in solidarity with Christ. This realisation enables Paul to see believers as previously corporately dead, in solidarity with the mythical Adam.[26] The reality of moral evil is too great to be accounted for purely socially, any more than by individual ill will. On the one hand, the reality of original sin seems evident in the light of human history. On the other hand, the evidence of science makes it difficult to believe in a pre-lapsarian state of nature in which human beings possessed preternatural as well as supernatural gifts. Rather, nature itself seems to have been cruel and savage, as well as beautiful and mysterious, from the beginning. St Paul's account of nature suffering like a woman giving birth[27] can be applied to a concurrent process of creation and redemption. From the first awakenings of human consciousness, human beings have failed to accept God's call, and this failure has had consequences for all the generations that have followed. Meanwhile, the acceptance of this call by Jesus has made the new solidarity possible.

Sharing in the life of the Trinity involves a new appreciation of every individual's worth as a person gratuitously loved and forgiven by God. Such a vision implies a radical equality between persons, which is at odds with the prevailing wisdom of society. Passivity in the face of the neglect of those in need and collusion with unjust economic and political systems is incompatible with the trinitarian perspective on equality with each other, in and with the one who became poor for our sakes.[28] By contrast, the economic and social system we inhabit applauds us when we become rich for our own

---

[25] Heinrich Denzinger, *Enchiridion symbolorum: definitionum et declarationum de rebus fidei et morum*, 32nd ed. *Quod primum edidit Henricus Denzinger et quod funditus retractavit, auxit, notulis, ornavit Adolfus Schönmetzer* (Barcinone: Herder, 1963), art. 3897, 780.

[26] 1 Cor. 15: 21-24.

[27] Rom. 8: 22.

[28] 2 Cor. 8: 9.

sakes, rather than poor for the sake of others. However, a proper understanding of the trinitarian perspective has the capacity to subvert such a value system. In Christ, the God of infinite strength and power is seen as involving himself in weakness and vulnerability, experiencing physical suffering, psychological desolation and death.[29] His solidarity with the poor and the weak is vindicated by the Father's action in raising him from the dead and pouring out the Holy Spirit on those who believe.[30]

In the Christian experience, Christ who is the way to God as Father is also the way towards a new human community. Although the new human community can only find its full realisation in the Kingdom, the gift is foreshadowed in every movement towards genuine human liberation, whether personal, social, economic, or political. The trinitarian understanding is capable of offering a vision of community based on loving reciprocity rather than aggressive competition. Translated into modern terms, it is difficult to see how anyone claiming to be a Christian can escape from the obligation to support practical social and political action that promotes the interests of the poor, the underprivileged, and the oppressed. The understanding of 'the preferential option for the poor' is rooted in the belief in Christ as God who has become human. Called and orientated towards union with God, the human person finds that there is a community of persons within God. Thus it is the task of the preacher to proclaim a call to union with God that is also a call to community.

---

[29] Phil. 2: 1-11.
[30] Acts 2: 32-36.

THE DOGMA IS THE DRAMA

Katherine C Calore

In the autumn of 1997, I was the vicar of a small mission congregation in my diocese. I was just a few months out of seminary, where I had unexpectedly discovered both a gift for and a passion for preaching. I was even at that point beginning to envision a time when I would no longer serve in parish ministry and could pursue my commitment to preaching full time, most likely as a seminary professor of homiletics. As I think about the past three years of my ministry, I realize that recent generations have seen a renewed joy in the sacramental element of our common life, which is a good thing and helps us recapture the fullness of our faith. Yet, there seems to be an understanding that one is there for the Eucharist and that the sermon is not really that important. I am convinced that this is the attitude of people who have been little touched or moved by the sermons they have heard and that this, to complete the circle, is in large part due to preachers who are inadequately trained or who themselves have little commitment to making preaching a priority in their ministry. My experience tells me that when a congregation is being fed a consistent diet of good sermons, suddenly preaching is much more important to them.

I heard from a friend, a fellow priest, of a Sunday this summer when he was on vacation and attended church with his parents. The Old Testament reading for the day was about the ten commandments, and the priest preached that the congregation was not required to take these laws seriously, since they were obviously too hard to keep. My friend's response to this was, 'Mom and Dad, you need to get yourself a new priest.' But this priest has never been censured or reprimanded, either by his congregation or his bishop, both of whom are responsible for seeing to it that the faith is truly preached in the Church's pulpits. This is a reflection of G K Chesterton's observation that 'The Christian faith has not been tried and found wanting. It has been found difficult and left untried.'

Faith's difficulty

I find that acknowledging the difficulty of a scriptural passage does far more to reach listeners than simply dismissing that passage out of hand. By pinning down my own discomfort with certain biblical passages and addressing my own struggle and making it bigger for my congregation, I am also addressing everyone else's struggle. The Christian faith is difficult, and I have found that people are profoundly grateful to hear a priest say it out loud. Yet the Christian faith is also saving, glorious, refining, and awesome, and I believe that I am in some cases the first priest to bring the drama of our Story to the pulpit. I firmly believe what Dorothy Sayers says: ' ... the dogma is the drama.'[1] It is dramatic, it is powerful and life-changing, and it is uncomfortable and painful and joyful, and those are not meek and mild sorts of adjectives. Dogma is worth getting worked up about. Sermons that minimize or deny the extremity, the drama, of the way of Christian discipleship do no service to the faith or to the people.

The self-proclaimed mission of the Episcopal Church is ' ... to restore all people to unity with God and each other in Christ.'[2] How is this to come about if nobody is telling those people why this unity is desirable or how their lives must change if we are to attain it? My own parish has a corresponding mission statement, 'To know Christ and to make Christ known.' I believe in these statements, and I believe that they both reflect the Great Commission and each individual's baptismal vows. Any personal mission or individual call must fall within the parameters set by these statements. I am committed to fulfilling this mission through my own striving toward holiness, in prayer most especially, and through acting faithfully within my circle of influence. That circle includes my family and friends, of course, but because I am a priest, it also includes several hundred other people. I am bound by my vows to proclaim what the Church teaches, and I am deeply glad to do so. I believe, along with Sayers:

> If the average man is going to be interested in Christ at all, it is the dogma that will provide the interest. The trouble is that, in nine cases out of ten, he has never been offered the dogma. What he has been offered is a set of technical terms that nobody has taken the trouble to translate into language relevant to ordinary life.[3]

---

[1] Dorothy L. Sayers, 'The Greatest Drama Ever Staged' in *The Whimsical Christian* (New York: Macmillan, 1978), 11.

[2] *Book of Common Prayer* (New York: Church Hymnal Corp., 1979), 855.

[3] Sayers, 'Creed or Chaos', in *The Whimsical Christian*, 39.

I have found this to be true in my experience. When I preach what some would call dry or academic or dull theology (for example, a Trinity Sunday sermon), I have person after person approach me to say, 'I never understood why we needed that before,' or 'It really does have something to do with real life, doesn't it?' They are excited by dogma because I am excited by dogma, and they hear it anew. This is the heart of my preaching ministry, because the dogma is a straight path to God in Christ, and I am committed to knowing Christ and making him known, and to reconciling all people with God and each other in Christ. As Mary Catherine Hilkert says, 'To offer others a new vision of reality, a new way of understanding and interpreting life, is in fact to offer them new life.'[4] That new life is, again, knowing Christ and making him known, and being reconciled to him and to each other in him.

These mission statements reflect an understanding which the Episcopal Church, indeed all of Anglicanism as a theological system, has of herself. It is part of our mythology, woven into our ethos and way of life, to consider ourselves 'plain vanilla Christianity'. This is to say, there is nothing distinctive to Anglicanism that is not distinctive to Christianity in general. Also referred to as 'mere Christianity', after the C S Lewis book of that title, the philosophy is that Roman Catholics have added things unnecessary to the simplicity of the faith (the Marian dogmas, papal infallibility), while Protestants have stripped away things necessary to the fullness of the faith (Marian devotion, the communion of saints, holy tradition). What is distinctively Anglican is the commitment to living in tension and seeking balance between two inadequate extremes; the *via media*, the middle way. Our mission is to restore all people to unity with God and each other in Christ, no more and no less.

Mere Christianity

The question, then, of an Anglican's operative theology will nearly always take place within that understanding of himself or herself, and of his or her ecclesiastical community. Most individual Anglicans, of course, stress certain parts of this 'mere Christianity', and some even ally themselves theologically with some *via* that is less *media* than the general Anglican approach, Calvinism or Ultramontanism, for example. I intend to discuss my understanding of my ministry within this Anglican context, but also to demonstrate which aspects of

---

[4] Mary Catherine Hilkert, *Naming Grace. Preaching and the Sacramental Imagination* (New York: Continuum, 1997), 97.

the tradition I feel must be stressed if the mission of the Church is to be met.

Christian dogma is complex and sophisticated, having been woven over two millennia from unplumbed depths of raw materials left to us by Jesus and his apostles. I said earlier that this dogma is the heart of my preaching ministry; it is, in fact, the heart of all my ministry. As an Anglican, I make a claim to the Christian faith, no more and no less, but that, then, begs the question: 'What do you mean by the Christian faith?'

For Anglicans, there is no single source to which one can appeal for the 'final answer'. Our sources are comprised of many complimentary books, documents, and accepted practices, the most important ones being Holy Scripture (Old and New Testaments, including the apocrypha), the *Book of Common Prayer* (all editions, with the most recent holding the most authority), the three great creeds (Apostles', Nicene, and Athanasian), the doctrinal pronouncements of the first seven ecumenical councils, the hymnal (which is thoroughly examined for doctrinal faithfulness before publication), and the teaching of our bishops and the collegial gathering at the triennial General Convention. It is from these sources, as well as from the writings of many ancient and contemporary saints and theologians, that I draw my theology, my Christology, and my anthropology.

My theology is trinitarian, incarnational, traditional, and liberal, and I think that I will have to begin this way, even though this beginning seems to use words that are so well-used as to have lost their meaning. The quest of the preacher, of course, is to restore the meaning. Hilkert's image of a spectrum between the dialectical Christian imagination and the sacramental Christian imagination is very helpful in the quest to make meaning from these worn words. In Anglican fashion, I perceive myself to strike a balance between these two imaginations, but I believe in the traditional understanding of God-for-us in such a way as to lean to the sacramental side of the Christian spectrum.

God requires much and is exacting and demanding, but God always knows that we are so bound up in our own sin that we are bound to fail, and continues to give and forgive nevertheless. God never runs out of second chances. The *Book of Common Prayer* asserts this over and over: 'Stir up your power, O Lord, and with great might come among us; and, because we are sorely hindered by our sins, let your bountiful grace and mercy speedily help and deliver us… .'[5] 'O God who wonderfully created, and yet more wonderfully restored, the dignity of human nature … '[6] 'Almighty and everlasting God, you are always more ready to hear than we are to pray, and to give more than

---

[5]   *Book of Common Prayer*, 212.
[6]   *Ibid.*, 214.

we either desire or deserve ... .'[7] There is a note of judgment, an acknowledgment of failure, but also a proclamation of God's grace overcoming even our sinfulness. Human failure notwithstanding, no separation between God and humanity is the final word. As Hilkert states it, 'What Christians celebrate is that death and evil do not have the final victory; the power of God does.'[8] This is true even in the most mundane details of our life. Even though our perception of revelation is clouded by our sin, God reveals himself to us through all of creation, including other sinful human beings. In some cases, the power of God is the power to make himself weak, or small, or dramatically limited so that we might perceive him. I am reminded of the story of St Martin of Tours where St Martin gives half his cloak to a beggar, then has a dream where Christ appears before his Father's throne dressed in the same cloak and claiming, 'Martin gave this cloak to me.' It is not that the beggar was Jesus in disguise; it was that in serving the beggar, Martin served Christ. This is a story of how anything can become a sacrament, a material vehicle for God's grace, if God chooses to use it that way.

When I say that my theology is trinitarian, I mean this in the most conservative and antique sense of that word. Oddly, it is a stance that puts me at variance with much contemporary theology, both Anglican and otherwise. I am committed to that convoluted Athanasian formulation of the trinitarian nature of God (though I find 'without doubt he shall perish everlastingly'[9] to be a little harsh)—though this creed clearly needs to be addressed by preachers from the pulpit in order for its doctrine to be appreciated. According to Douglas John Hall, 'The trouble was (and is) that as a positive statement of the identity of God in Christian belief, the trinitarian formula never functioned well.'[10] He is right in the sense that the classical doctrine of the Trinity, complete with complex Greek grammar, is the best articulation of what was left after the Church weeded out the unacceptable alternatives. He is also right in the sense that our best articulation has not gone very far in helping Christians get our minds around this dogma. When our best articulation does little to help us get our minds around our own central dogma, we should be humbly aware that God does not fit our limited grasp, and be grateful for it as well. As Sara Maitland puts it, 'The desire to reduce it all to a tidy little formula is irresistible and must be resisted: in the last count why bother about a tiny little, simple God who is slightly less complicated than the workings of my

---

[7]   *Ibid.*, 234.

[8]   Hilkert, 116.

[9]   *Quicunque Vult*, commonly called 'The Creed of Saint Athanasius', *Book of Common Prayer,* 864.

[10] Douglas John Hall, *Professing the Faith: Christian Theology in a North American Context* (Minneapolis: Fortress, 1993), 69.

own mind?'[11] In our long-lived tradition of the Trinity, we have certainly come up with a formula, but it is, as Hall says, so sprawling and untidy that it does not work well as a positive statement of the identity of God. It works superbly as a negative one, however, which is sufficient to ensure that we are worshipping Yahweh and no other, and leaves the rest of the mystery alive between us. Hall does not question the truth to which the dogma points, but he does speculate about the continued usefulness of the formula we cling to in order to explain that mysterious truth: 'Trinitarian theology is not served well … by those who simply repeat that God is "Father, Son, and Holy Spirit."'[12] He makes that assertion because he believes that the Nicene understanding of this dogma has 'no existential basis in contemporary consciousness.'[13] Yet, it seems to be the very task of the preacher to build a bridge between the ancient formulas and contemporary consciousness. If the Trinity, whether formula or underlying reality, is n relevant to contemporary consciousness, perhaps some of the responsibility for this rests on those preachers who have been unable to express the importance of the truth itself, and so unable to foster a relationship between the people and the triune God. If so, a trinitarian formula which does have 'existential basis in contemporary consciousness' is still unlikely to succeed, because any such approach would be lacking the underlying commitment to the very God a new formula attempted to represent.

An inseparable aspect of the dogma of the Trinity is the dogma of the incarnation, and it is this central dogma which makes all of Christian life sacramental with dialectical aspects, rather than the other way around. Material life is sacred because the Word of God took on matter, became material, for the sake of his material creatures. Material existence is not God, but it is the artwork of God and can reveal and communicate God to those who seek his revelation. St Teresa of Avila asserts somewhat sarcastically: 'This withdrawal from the corporeal must doubtless be good, since it is advised by such spiritual people, but my belief is that it must be practised only when the soul is very proficient; until then, it is clear, the Creator must be sought through the creatures.'[14]

The incarnation is the ultimate demonstration of the fact that God can and does work through anything to communicate with us, to be near us,

---

[11] Sara Maitland, *A Big-Enough God: A Feminist's Search for a Joyful Theology* (New York: Holt, 1995), 2.

[12] Hall, 72.

[13] *Ibid.*, 9.

[14] Teresa of Avila, *The Life of the Holy Mother Teresa of Jesus*, ch. 22, esc. 8, in *The Complete Works of Saint Teresa of Jesus*, vol. 1, ed. and trans. E Allison Peers (London/New York: Sheed and Ward, 1950), 139.

to draw us nearer to him. God could no longer tolerate the degree of separation between himself and us, even though that separation was brought on by our own sin. This idea that God seeks us out and reveals himself to us in the mundane material things of life is so important to the task of preaching.

While the idea of God-with-us or God-for-us is expressive to both dialectical and sacramental Christian imaginations, my Anglican leaning remains toward the sacramental imagination. Mary Catherine Hilkert describes the sacramental imagination in the following words:

> The sacramental imagination (or what Tracy calls the analogical imagination) emphasizes the presence of the God who is self-communicating love, the creation of human beings in the image of God (restless hearts seeking the divine), the mystery of the incarnation, grace as divinizing as well as forgiving, the mediating role of the Church as sacrament of salvation in the world, and the "foretaste" of the reign of God that is present in the human community wherever God's reign of justice, peace, and love is fostered.[15]

This is not, of course, to ignore the horrors of suffering, or even the mundanities of suffering experienced so often by so many, and Hilkert spends several chapters addressing those very difficulties within the context of sacramental Christianity. It is to say, however, that God's grace is 'divinizing as well as forgiving', that God chose first to be present to us in our created nature and human experience, even as he now pronounces his compassionate and transcendent 'nevertheless' to human sin.

Douglas John Hall claims that the dogma of the incarnation articulated at Chalcedon, too, was reached through a negative process, through 'trial and error and in the confusion of motives that always accompanies intense religious struggles.'[16] I agree that this is another case in which we perhaps can only say that the alternatives are unacceptable and so assert the one statement left after culling out all the others. But it seems inadequate to say that the possibilities engendered when God and humanity meet uniquely in the person of Jesus Christ must remain a mystery. It seems to me, in fact, that the whole Christian enterprise is specifically about plumbing the depths of that mystery, about fitting our life into that Life. Hall states that for faith, '[Jesus'] humanity defines authentic humanity and not the other way around,'[17] but if we are to allow our humanity to be moulded to conform to his, then

---

[15] Hilkert, 15.
[16] Hall, 400.
[17] *Ibid.*, 403.

we must explore the very mystery we are allowing to define us. The incarnation is very particular, and if Jesus' humanity is to determine my humanity, then I have to know how, and I have to know what changes will have to be made to my life if I want it to look like his. It's not a hands-off, we can never understand it, sort of mystery. It's a hands-on, roll up your sleeves, get sweaty and dirty and bloody, what do I do now, sort of mystery. It was for Jesus, and it will be no less for us. It is different in this way from the dogma of the Trinity, an essential purpose of which is to identify God's unknowability. The incarnation teaches us exactly the opposite truth, God's consenting to be known in the only life we have in which to know anything.

Changing our lives

Returning to my earlier assertion of the inherent drama of Christian dogma, it is in Christology, or the dogma of the incarnation, where some of this drama plays itself out. It is quite shocking to most people to hear Christian dogma portrayed as something so intense and wild that people would— literally if you can credit it—die for it. So, to unequivocally assert traditional Christology from the pulpit can cause some problems for the preacher. After all, it has in the past made people so angry that they had to have those Christians preaching it killed. Dorothy Sayers says the following:

> First, I believe it to be a grave mistake to present Christianity as something charming and popular with no offense in it. Seeing that Christ went about the world giving the most violent offense to all kinds of people, it would seem absurd to expect that the doctrine of his person can be so presented as to offend nobody. We cannot blink at the fact that gentle Jesus, meek and mild, was so stiff in his opinions and so inflammatory in his language that he was thrown out of church, stoned, hunted from place to place, and finally gibbeted as a firebrand and a public danger. Whatever his peace was, it was not the peace of an amiable indifference; he said in so many words that what he brought with him was fire and sword. That being so, nobody need be too surprised or disconcerted that a determined preaching of Christian dogma may sometimes result in a few angry letters of protest or a difference of opinion on the parish council.[18]

I am convinced, like Sayers, that a faithful preaching of the Gospel will always offend someone, and I am quite satisfied to stir up this sort of

---

[18] Sayers, 'Creed or Chaos', 42.

drama in the congregation, provided it is done for the sake of the dogma, and not in service to the drama itself.

I am drawn to the drama of the dogma, in part, because of factors I have already mentioned concerning my understanding of human nature. Simply put, I believe that people are good, but are prone to sin. By sin I mean not only wrong actions, but also wrong character which comes from separation from God. I am occasionally compelled to shake things up a bit because I am well aware that people in general are prone to complacency. I frequently preach doctrine, dependent on the lectionary, in order to counter that thoughtless sincerity which can pull us from the paths of truth in the name of niceness. There are few things people can do or say to shock me ('You can't shock the clergy'), but it is our quiet sins, those woven-in ways of living for ourselves rather than for God and others, which distress and discourage me most about fallen human nature. Most of the time I see people as pretty decent, doing the best that they can. Sometimes I see them as desperate, pathetic, more deeply needy than they even realize. I am always aware that God may come to me in any person I encounter. But more and more often, I am concerned lest we Anglicans sell short our ancient faith by modifying it to fit our contemporary lives, out of an unwillingness to change our lives to conform to our faith. This concern might seem harsh, because selling short is usually done with good intentions and deeply felt sincerity. Yet, the point of the priesthood and of our preaching is not to spare our parishioners' feelings at the expense of calling them to the demands of authentic discipleship.

In good Anglican fashion, I find myself living in the tension between being both critical and celebratory of Anglicans and Anglicanism. I celebrate the empowering and gracious gifts of this heritage. It is why I became an Anglican in the first place. But I find that the Episcopal Church and other western churches are falling prey to those quiet sins which plague the human condition. In this case, that quiet sin is the sin of knowing better. For us this sin causes us to disregard two millennia (and more) of faithful life and worship in favour of a 're-imaged' faith which suits our lives better. It never occurs to us to change our lives to suit the faith. I am not saying, nor would I say, that all the generations that came before us were right, and ours is wrong. I am saying that we have much to learn from our brothers and sisters of ages past, and we should tread with great humility when we seek, as occasionally we must, to change what they have handed down. This does not come naturally to a community bound, as all are, by sin, but it is the work of God to free us from those bonds. Our tradition has bestowed so many life-giving gifts upon us, including a tradition of powerful preaching, and we may find that we return these gracious gifts only at great cost to ourselves and to those we seek to restore to unity with God and each other in Christ.

UWA NA-ASO,
THE WORLD IS SWEET

Linus Ebele Edogwo

An Igbo proverb states that whoever gets up from their seat has a purpose or a destination in mind. Igbo (sometimes spelt Ibo) people regard as insane those who do not know where they are going or their purpose for getting up from their seat. For this reason, it is important to me to think about where I am going as a preacher if I am to be so bold as to get up into the pulpit.

Different preachers understand preaching in different ways. For a priest friend of mine, borrowing from the gospel account of the sower, preaching is the planting of God's seeds. In this sense, the preacher is seen as the farmer. He plants the seeds, waters and nurtures them till they yield fruits in harvest time. One of the striking images in this description is the patience and diligence of the farmer who toils under sunshine and rainfall for a harvest he is not sure he will live to see.

In its definition of preaching, *The American Heritage College Dictionary* uses such phrases as 'to proclaim or put forth a sermon'; 'to advocate, especially, to urge acceptance for or compliance with'; 'to give religious or moral instruction, especially in a tedious manner'. One wonders the reason for the writer's use of the words 'tedious manner' in the definition. Perhaps he or she may have experienced some boring preachers on pretty regular occasions.

However, the above definition calls to mind certain images about the act of preaching and the person of a preacher. For instance, the word 'proclaim' presents the preacher as a prophet, 'to put forth' calls to mind the idea of giving birth, perhaps to new meaning of life, while the word 'advocate' stands for one who pleads a case as opposed to another who commands or enforces an order.

Following Paul's description of a preacher as an ambassador, C H Spurgeon insists that a preacher is sent, not to proclaim his own words, but those of the one who sent him, since 'the very soul of the ambassadorial office lies in the appointment which is made by the monarch represented.'[1]

---

[1]   C H Spurgeon, *Lectures to My Students* (London: Marshall Morgan and Scott, 1982), 24.

The authenticity of the ambassador ceases if the preacher goes beyond this commissioned mandate. Hall's notion of 'representative' certainly adds the additional role of preacher as speaker for the people of God.[2]

In Igbo traditional religion, the priest stands as a messenger of God. He is bound by his office to represent the people before God through presenting their prayers, feelings, opinions, and sacrifices to God, as well as bringing God's messages to the people. Any mistake consciously or unconsciously on his part was taken seriously by the deity he serves. For instance, my paternal grandfather, Chief Edogwo Epundu was a high priest of Udoh. He was said to have been struck fatally ill after he mistakenly ate a piece of the cola nuts he offered as part of a sacrifice to Udoh on behalf of a woman worshiper.

I see preaching as the most essential part of the Church's life and ministry. The Church can hardly survive without preaching. We can define preaching as the sharing of the divine mystery of grace and hope, whether in words or deeds, with and among God's people. It is sharing, in the sense that both the preacher and the audience are benefited in the preaching event. God is at the centre of preaching. A preaching event is essentially dialogical in the sense that the people's experiences help to shape and reshape theology or our understanding of God. After studying theology for four years, I was ordained in 1986. My first assignment was to assist another priest for two years in a remote parish in Nigeria. My contact with the poor peasant farmers in preaching and other pastoral activities gave me a unique understanding of God I never learnt in the seminary.

When I think of preaching, the image that often comes to my mind is that of my maternal grandfather who was the best wine taper in his village. As a tropical country, one of the commonest trees in Nigeria is the palm. In fact, it is the most important tree in Igboland. Igbo people use every part of the tree for one thing or another. For instance, palm oil is extracted from the fruits and the kernel. The shell is used as power supply for cooking, and the leaves are used for feeding domestic animals like sheep and goats, while the stem is split up and used for roofing houses. Above all, palm wine, which was the major alcohol served at various occasions and celebrations came from the sap, which flowed in the centre of the palm stem.

A lot of hard work was involved before one could get the sap from the palm tree. I recall my grandfather first clearing a good part of the leaves from their buds on top of the tree. Then he would cut off some part of the upper stem from a side. Then finally he would carefully bore a hole from the

---

2   Douglas John Hall, *Professing the Faith: Christian Theology in a North American Context* (Minneapolis: Fortress, 1993), 509.

side he cleared into the centre of the stem. In doing this he would be careful not to cut too little or too much, as doing so would prevent the flow of the sap. The quantity and taste of the wine often, though not definitely, depended on the skill and expertise of the taper. My grandfather drank very little, but his greatest happiness was to see people enjoy his wine at various celebrations.

This story about my grandfather may not be a perfect analogy, but it always helps me to remember that I have a major part to play in the way people receive or react to the Word of God. Just like my grandfather's palm wine, the taste of my homily will depend, to a large extent, on how well and carefully I have prepared for it. Following the above analogy, the preaching act here includes the various occasions and celebrations in the village with all the deliberations, debates, stories, reflections (as during marriages, village festivals, reconciliation, and new births), and tears (as at funerals). These form an essential part of the villagers as a people, and what they think about themselves and about God.

The Igbo sense of the sacred

The Igbo culture in which I was born and raised has a very high sense of the sacred. This was an essential part of the life of the people that some of the early missionaries to Nigeria, as well as western writers, failed to understand. Thus they considered every religious belief of the local people as superstition and idol worship. Some of them argued that the idea of God was too sophisticated for the uneducated African mind to comprehend. They referred to the people as pagans and heathens. But a close look at the life and culture of Igbo people, as well as many other African communities, shows their highly rooted sense of God. For instance, a British Anglican missionary and anthropologist who spent fourteen years studying the Igbo culture wrote: 'Among the Igbo people there is a distinct recognition of a Supreme being— beneficent in character—who is above every other spirit, good or evil. He is believed to control all things in heaven and on earth, and dispenses rewards and punishments according to merit.'[3]

The above, in a sense, summarizes the theology of Igbo people. There is only one God. This supreme being who we call *Chukwu* in our language is responsible for the existence of other beings in the world. He made humankind, the trees, the mountains, the seas, the animals, in fact, everything—both those we see and those we do not see. The characteristics

---

[3] G T Basden, *Among the Igbos of Nigeria* (London: Frank Cass, 1966), 215.

of the supreme being in Igbo traditional religion definitely correspond with the spirit of the beatitudes as seen in Christian theology.

Contrary to the opinion of some philosophers, God did not just create the world and abandon it to its fate. He rather sustains it at every moment. Thus God's creation of the world is a continuous process. This idea is very strongly expressed in several Igbo myths. According to Metuh: 'These myths emphasize that Chukwu is the creator and organizer of the universe. ... He made night and day and arranged them into the four-day week of the Igbo. Thus not only the material world but also its most important attributes—space, time, and order were introduced and controlled by Chukwu.'[4]

In spite of the unity in the supreme being, there are three divine persons—Father, Son, and Holy Spirit. This is what is known in Christian theology as the Trinity. The idea of the Trinity has no explicit derivative in Igbo traditional religion. The closest we have is the idea of the deities who are considered as God's representatives and intermediaries between God and humankind. The deities are considered powerful, but they are not supreme beings. They only exercise limited control over humankind and human affairs as much as *Chukwu* gives them the power to do so.

Our inability to give adequate explanation of the Trinity, which would make sense to modern thought, does not in any way render it incredible or meaningless. Moreover, the difficulty encountered in our efforts to understand the Trinity and other issues about God calls for openness of mind, not only among various church denominations, but also among different world religions.

The nature and essence of the supreme being is beyond human comprehension. If we as human beings are capable of understanding God, then he ceases to be the supreme being. Yet, our inability to understand his essence does not render his existence null and void. He is God, living and true, whether we know him or otherwise. He does not need us in order to be fulfilled in himself. God's existence is not scientifically or empirically proven. It is mainly a matter of faith. What we do in theology is to give some reasons to our faith in order to articulate and sustain our belief in God. Without faith, there is neither religion nor theology.

One of the ways to acquire some kind of knowledge of God is through his attributes. In other words, God could somehow be known through what he does. The Igbo names for God explain this idea very clearly. For instance, *Chukwu* is a combination of two words *Chi* (God) and *ukwu* (great)—

---

[4] Emefie I Metuh, *African Religions in Western Conceptual Schemes* (Ibadan: Claverianum, 1985), 40.

in other words, 'the Great God'. Another name, *Chineke*, means the 'God who creates', and *Olisa-bulu-uwa* means the 'God who carries or sustains the world'. One of the songs we were taught as children helps to illustrate this point: '*Uwa na-aso, uwa na-aso, Chukwu selu aka, uwa agwu.*' This translates, 'The world is sweet, the world is sweet, but when God removes his hand, the world is finished.'

The Igbo ideas about *Chukwu* could also be seen from Igbo proverbs. For instance, '*Odighi ihe gbara Chukwu ghari,*' means, 'Nothing is a surprise to God.' In other words, God is capable of everything. '*Chukwu nwe ndu onye na-efu ohia,*' means, 'God owns the life of the one who is lost in the forest.' This shows not only the faith of Igbo people, but also their trust in the almighty power of the supreme being.

As Basden noted, Igbo people believe that as the supreme being, God has at his service many ministering spirits whose sole business is to fulfil his command. This corresponds with the Christian idea of angels whose function the Bible describes as ministering to God day and night. Igbo people feel that God is too great and awesome, so that doing certain things would be too mean for a being on such high pedestal. But this does not imply that God needs the services or worship of the angels in order to be God. He is still God, whether the angels minister to him or not. Human beings are also supposed to worship God on earth as the angels do in heaven. This brings us to the next consideration: who is humanity?

Humanity as the beauty of life

Beginning from the ancient times, many people have tried in various ways to address the question of the nature of the human person. The Greek philosophers approached the issue in a number of ways. Prominent among these philosophers was Plato who proposed the duality of humanity as made up of body and soul. He described the relationship between the body and the soul as constantly in direct opposition to each other. Aristotle and others took up Plato's dualism.

In the Middle Ages, everything was explained with reference to God. Everything material, including the human person, was condemned, and the platonic idea of freeing the soul from the body was a common philosophy. The Church was the sole authority, not only in matters of faith and morals, but also in social and political life. God was seen both as the creator and solution to every human problem. In the Renaissance, however, everything changed. The authority of God and the Church was challenged to a very great extent. Humanity became the focus of study and the focus for finding solutions to problems. Human reason was exalted, and humanity's capacity and ability were seen as infinite.[5]

Plato's position about the nature of the human person as body and soul and about the consequence of such composition on human nature has influenced many writers across the ages. Writing on the nature of humanity, William Shakespeare gave what I consider to be one of the best passages in his entire works:

> What a piece of work is a man, how noble in reason, how infinite in faculties, in form and moving, how express and admirable in action, how like an angel in apprehension, how like god! The beauty of the world; the paragon of animals; and yet to me what is this quintessence of dust?[6]

Shakespeare expresses the dual composition of humankind in a very striking way. We thus can see that humanity has both positive and negative aspects. Theologically speaking, we can say that humanity has the ability for good and evil. The dual composition of humanity has influenced theology in some unfortunate ways. By this I mean that some theologians have emphasized one aspect of the human person as against the other. Following Plato, who also posited that the soul is imprisoned in the body, many theologians argue that the body is incapable of doing anything good. It does not matter how much the soul tries to get away from the body; it is still held in bondage. In this way, humanity is seen as intrinsically evil. This is the idea we read from Genesis, where the fall of Adam and Eve basically destroyed the relationship between God and humanity. The original sin is presented as having pervaded the whole of humanity. Emphasizing the soul aspect of humanity presents human nature as only good. It loses sight of the evils that abound in the world today.

I once asked my father, Mr Eugene Edogwo, the origin of the word *mmadu*, the Igbo for humankind. He explained that etymologically the word *mmadu* is a combination of two words, *mma* (beauty) and *ndu* (life). Put together, therefore, it means the beauty of life. Igbo people, and many other African cultures, see humanity as good, since humankind is the beauty of life.

Writing on Igbo worldview, Metuh states: 'The world of human experience is seen as one fluid coherent unit in which spirits, men, animals, plants, and the elements are engaged in continuous interaction.'[7]

---

[5]   G R Potter, *The New Cambridge Modern History* (Cambridge: Cambridge University Press, 1957), 74.

[6]   William Shakespeare, *Hamlet*, 2.2.337.

[7]   Metuh, 38.

Humankind is seen not just as a part of this unit but at the centre of it. The world is grossly incomplete without humanity. As Mbiti observed, 'Man is at the very centre of existence and African people see everything else in its relation to this central position of man.'[8]

The Igbos believe that humanity came from God. Thus God is both the origin and end of humankind. The details of how God created humanity differ from one Igbo group to another. Yet, the idea of the divine origin of humanity is not debated among the Igbos. As Metuh writes: 'Man in Igbo thought can be viewed from different perspectives. Viewed from the standpoint of his origin and final destiny, man is best understood in relation to Chukwu. Man comes from God. He has a definite mission to fulfil in God's plan and he will eventually go back to God.'[9]

Several Igbo personal names and proverbs also reflect humanity's origin from God. For instance, the name *Onyeneke* means 'who else creates'. This implies that God is the only creator. *Madueke* means 'humanity does not create'. Again, *Chukwukere* means 'God creates', and *Ekechukwu* is 'God's creature'. Humanity's dependence on God is illustrated in such proverbs as '*Onye buru chi ya uzo, O gbagbue onwe ya n'oso*' (If one tries to run faster than one's God, one runs to one's death), '*Onye ya na chi ya yi, ihe anaghi eme ya*' (One with one's God is above all harm), and '*Chukwu ji mma, jide ji, onye O wanyere, O rie*' (God holds both the knife and the yam, only those he slices a bit can eat). In other words, all power belongs to God alone.

Writing under the title 'Man, Family and Community', Metuh observes: 'Igbos, like most African people, define a person in terms of the group to which he belongs. A Person is thought of first of all as a member of a particular family, kindred, clan, or tribe. The family is made up of not only one's living relatives at the widest possible scope, but also the dead members and those yet to be born.'[10]

The above certainly corresponds with the Christian idea of the communion of the saints. The emphasis on communal life has been described by many writers of both African and western origin as the basis for the survival of the African race, especially in view of the deplorable economic condition ravaging almost the entire African continent.

In *Naming Grace*, Mary Catherine Hilkert expresses concern lest theologians or preachers of sacramental imagination be so preoccupied with

---

[8] John S Mbiti, *African Religions and Philosophy* (New York: Frederick A Prager, 1969), 92.

[9] Metuh Ikenga Metuh, *God and Man in African Religion* (London: Geoffrey Chapman, 1981), 5.

[10] *Ibid.*, 99.

humankind in the image of God that they forget our fallen nature.[11] Today many preachers in our churches hardly mention the fallen state of humanity. Very rarely do we hear homilies about sin, hell, or various evils committed by human beings in the world, such as racism, ageism, sexism, numerous violent crimes against women and children, and other forms of inhumanity. Effective preaching must not exclude, but rather come to terms with, what Hilkert and Phyllis Trible describe as 'texts of terror'.[12] The human condition, in both its grace and its disgrace, must be emphasized from the pulpit. To preach on only smooth things, and to extenuate the evil of our lost estate, is grossly insufficient to lead humanity to God. A true and authentic view of the nature of humanity must include both the positive and the negative aspects. There are sin and evil in human nature, but we have been raised to a divine level through the grace of God (*ebelechukwu*), which has been made visible, like Paul said, through the divine Son of God—Jesus the Christ.

Chukwunonye (God-with-us)

Christians are very much divided as to who Jesus is. This is no surprise, in view of the uniqueness of his being and message.

In spite of the efforts of the councils of Nicaea (325), Ephesus (431), and Chalcedon (451), christology has remained a crucial problem in the Church to this day. But, as Douglas John Hall insists, any authentic christology must bear in mind two fundamental principles: 'first, that this person must be regarded as having been a genuinely human being, whose real humanity must not be sacrificed for the sake of accentuating or seeming to accentuate faith's claims to his ultimacy; second, that this person must be regarded as being uniquely related to the being and purposing of God.'[13] To put it in simple language, there is no dispute about the existence of Jesus as a historical person. There is also little debate about the fact that he taught some new doctrines to his followers, and that later he had problems with some Roman and Jewish authorities and was subsequently condemned and executed by crucifixion. However, the great controversy about Jesus centres on what happened after his death.

The resurrection of Jesus is the focal point of Christianity. Unfortunately this important event cannot be historically or scientifically proven. It is purely a matter of faith. An authentic and complete christology

---

[11] Mary Catherine Hilkert, *Naming Grace: Preaching and the Sacramental Imagination* (New York: Continuum, 1997), 19-45.

[12] *Ibid.*, 75.

[13] Hall, 394.

must include Jesus' death on the cross and his resurrection from the dead. For Paul, the yardstick for measuring the authenticity of a preacher is the cross of Christ. But we should not talk about the cross without the resurrection, neither should we talk about the resurrection without the cross. It is the resurrection that gives meaning to the event of the cross. It is, however, significant to note that after Jesus rose from the dead only those who had faith in him saw him. Similarly, today only those who have faith believe in the resurrection. Christians, therefore, affirm that the second person of the Trinity is both the Jesus of history and the Christ of faith.[14]

The redemptive aspect of the second person of the Trinity is very much expressed in Igbo traditional religion, though not in the same way as in Christianity. Igbo people value the first male child in a family, as he directly inherits the father's estate when the father dies. A man who has no male child would do almost anything to get one. Childlessness or the inability to get a male child is one of the major reasons for polygamy in Igbo and African societies. The emphasis on children is clearly seen in some Igbo personal names like *Nwadimkpa* (A child is very essential), *Nwamaka* (A child is beautiful), *Nwadiugwu* (A child is dignifying), and *Nwakaego* (A child is more precious than money). These are only a few of Igbo names extolling the importance of children in Igbo culture.

Unfortunately, many western writers, in their efforts to express God's transcendence in Igbo traditional religion, failed to understand that Igbo culture is highly cognizant of God's immanence. This is seen in such personal names as *Chukwunonye* (God-with-us). It is the same as the Christian idea of Emmanuel.

The notion of sacrifice is a common one in Igbo traditional religion, though many authors argue that the sacrifices are made to deities rather than to God. Francis Arinze, however, emphasizes that in many parts of Igboland, sacrifices are made to the supreme being.[15] Even in places where the sacrifices are made to the deities, these deities often stand only as intermediaries and not the final recipients. The purposes of the sacrifices include thanksgiving, atonement for past offenses, petition for protection and new favours. In view of this, the Igbos do not find it difficult to relate to the idea that Jesus, God's only son, died for our sins.

God's public agreement with the poor

As the Church in Igboland not only takes roots but continues to grow at a

---

[14] Thomas Zanzig, *Jesus of History, Christ of Faith* (Winona, MN: St. Mary's, 1999), 16.
[15] Francis A Arinze, *Sacrifice in Ibo Religion* (Ibadan: University Press, 1970), 5.

great speed, preachers should constantly be aware of the great responsibility God has placed on their shoulders. Effective preaching in an Igbo context should take cognisance of the depth of the resources available in Igbo culture and traditional religion. Rather than 'throwing away the baby with the bath water', as the early missionaries did, today's preachers in Igboland should harness the rich resources in terms of knowledge, faith, wisdom, and dedication to God in the life of our ancestors. Only then can they satisfy the hunger and thirst of God's children, many of whom in Igboland travel for miles on foot to listen to the Word of life.

Today's Gospel should be interpreted in such a way as to explain its relevance to the lives of Igbo people. Any interpretation of the Gospel that neglects or, worse still, makes a mockery of the lives of many generations of the Igbo people who lived in the past will not have much meaning to the present-day Igbos.

As a result of the present economic depression in Nigeria, where the average monthly income per family is less than a hundred dollars, many families are finding it increasingly difficult to feed themselves two times a day. The rate of unemployment is higher than 38 percent, and more than 42 percent of college graduates are unemployed. Effective preaching must address the plight of the poor who form more than 70 percent of the population. In the Gospel, Jesus made love for God and for neighbour the centre of his ministry. Long before the advent of Christianity in Igboland, the survival of the Igbos as a people depended, to a very great extent, on various ways through which the Igbos took care of themselves and one another. Unfortunately, under the heavy burden of the present economic situation and the human instinct for self-preservation, many Igbos have forsaken the basis for the survival and success of our ancestors. They have not only abandoned the practice of charity that was the hallmark of the past Igbo generations, but they have gone on to exploit their sisters and brothers.

An Igbo proverb says that it is hard to sing alleluia on an empty stomach. The Church, through her preachers, should pay more attention to the suffering of the people and find ways to improve their condition. As Aloysius Pieris wrote about the Asian church: 'The story of God's public agreement with the poor to embark on the common task of transforming this world into a new heaven and a new earth that God and the poor are dreaming of together, is the story the Asians would never refuse to hear; and it is the story the Christians fear to narrate. And yet that story is Jesus.'[16]

Similarly, the Igbos will always welcome a Gospel that addresses

---

[16] Aloysius Pieris, 'Inter-Religious Dialogue and Theology of Religions: An Asian Paradigm', *East Asian Pastoral Review* 29:4 (1992): 375.

their suffering in the present Nigerian economic order, a Gospel that extols the positive beliefs and practices of our ancestors. Only such a Gospel will really be good news to the present Igbo race.

LISTEN TO MY SIGHING

James Hayes

The note is suspended, solitary. It is followed by a haunting soprano voice lamenting the loss of her son. He, in turn, offers hope:

> No, Mother, do not weep,
> Most chaste Queen of Heaven
> Support me always.
> *Zdrowas Mario.*[1]

Hers was a hope born of sorrow.

I agonize whenever I listen to Henryk Gorecki's thoroughly modern, simplistic *Symphony Number 3*. The music, which describes the horror of a mother whose son has died in a Nazi concentration camp, has become a part of my Good Friday observance. Dawn Upshaw's distinctive soprano allows neither solution to the heartbreak, nor the despair of a broken spirit. The utterance of this dignified woman, the narrator of the heartbreak and hope, is a sigh—an expression of sadness and yearning. Her sorrowful sigh is both realistic and hopeful.

Realism and hope are the foundation of my operative theology of preaching. The entire project revolves around the aforementioned metaphor of a sigh, which is understood here as a long, deep, and audible breath expressive of sadness, yet replete with longing and yearning. Any theology must confront

---

[1] Henryk Gorecki, *Symphony Number 3, Opus 36,* recorded May 1991 by London Sinfonietta, conducted by David Zinman, featuring Dawn Upshaw, Soprano (New York: Elektra Nonesuch, 1992). Gorecki begins the 'Symphony of Sorrowful Songs' with the fifteenth century *Lamentation of the Holy Cross*, depicting a mother's grief over her son's wounds. The second part of the sung text, quoted here, was a prayer inscribed on wall 3 of cell number 3 in the basement of the 'Palace', the Gestapo's headquarters in Zakopane. Beneath the prayer is the signature of Helena Wanda Blazusiakowma and the words: '18 years old, imprisoned since 26 September 1944'. *Zdrowas Mario* is translated 'Hail Mary'.

the reality of suffering and resulting sadness while articulating the hopeful yearning for the fullness of God's ever present reign.

Theological anthropology

> *Hear my words, O Lord;*
> *Listen to my sighing.*
> Ps. 5: 2 *NAB*

To begin with this category is thoroughly modern. My theology as a Roman Catholic who studied exclusively in seminaries of my own tradition has been influenced greatly by the work of Karl Rahner. The starting point of his theological project is 'The Hearer of the Message'.[2] To commence with the human person opens the theological project to Hans Küng's requirement that an effective theology be *critical* and *ecumenical*.[3] The postmodern world recognizes the influence of distinct intellectual and philosophical horizons, while maintaining the possibility of reflecting upon lived experiences as distinct. It is in the nature of human beings to consider their existence.[4] All persons, regardless of religious or spiritual background, are capable of reflecting critically on their experience. This is an experience of longing. The human person constantly searches for contentment or happiness—what the Greeks called well-being. Desire is stronger than satisfaction and is experienced as 'aching pain or delicious hope'.[5] The metaphor of a sigh as the lens through which this paper regards theological anthropology captures the sense of longing in the human heart. As we search for happiness or wellbeing, we often are disappointed. Nothing fulfills our apparently transcendent longing. As Rahner understands it, by our reflection on the self, motivated by longing, we give evidence to transcendent possibility. In this reflection or search, 'man [the

---

[2] Karl Rahner, *Foundations of Christian Faith: An Introduction to the Idea of Christianity*, trans. William V Dych (New York: Crossroad, 1986), 24.

[3] Hans Küng, *Theology for the Third Millennium* (New York: Doubleday, 1988), 161-62.

[4] Joseph M Webb, *Preaching and the Challenge of Pluralism,* (St Louis: Chalice, 1998). Webb, in chapters 1-3, elucidates the capacity of human beings to 'symbolize' and 'define' our existence in different ways, while recognizing that we come to beloved conclusions about who we are and what is valuable through the universal practice of reflection upon our 'hub symbols'.

[5] Ronald Rolheiser, *The Holy Longing: The Search for a Christian Spirituality* (New York: Doubleday, 1999), 5. Rolheiser's work has influenced my thoughts on anthropology in the area of spirituality and describes the longing of the human heart more clearly than this short anthropological section.

human person] is affirming himself as more than the sum of such analyzable components of his reality.'[6] This type of reflection by the longing heart requires some type of transcendent referent, which I choose to classify as God. Thus, anthropology as the starting point for a theology of preaching. The sigh in my own heart is known and capable of definition and points, though imperfectly, to the object of my desire.

Anthropology as a starting point for theology implies a 'sacramental imagination'.[7] All creation, not only the human person, points analogically or sacramentally to the grandeur of the creator. Though only creatures, human beings as the *imago dei*, uniquely engage this sacramental imagination as we attempt to give a name to the groaning of our hearts. Heart, in this instance, is used in the Hebrew sense as the symbol of the totality of the human person. The sacramentality of the *imago dei* in the human is experienced in the classical attributes of reason and free will, as well as in Douglas John Hall's attributes of 'gentleness, sacrificial love, compassion, humility, modesty, awe, responsibility for others, meekness, or gratitude … '.[8]

This optimistic description of the human person, though true, does not capture the totality of human nature which Martin Luther would claim is *simul justus et peccator*. As Hall notes: 'It would be questionable for faith to underestimate the radicality of evil in the name of a positive doctrine of creation … '.[9] A realistic understanding of human nature must take sin into account. Reinhold Niebuhr expressed this Christian realism as well as any other dialectical advocate of the twentieth century: 'Sin is occasioned precisely by the fact that man refuses to admit his "creatureliness" and to acknowledge himself as merely a member of a total unity of life. He pretends to be more than he is.'[10]

Recognition of the concept and reality of sin naturally tempers and corrects an overly optimistic theological anthropology. Human nature is appropriately defined, evil and the narratives of horror instigated by humanity are possible, and the need for redemption (central to the dialectical imagination) is recognized as necessary. The very existence of creation is dependent upon the grace-filled breath of God.

---

[6] Rahner, 29.

[7] Mary Catherine Hilkert, *Naming Grace: Preaching and the Sacramental Imagination* (New York: Continuum, 1997).

[8] Douglas John Hall, *Professing the Faith: Christian Theology in a North American Context* (Minneapolis: Fortress, 1993), 267.

[9] *Ibid.*, 198.

[10] Reinhold Niebuhr, *The Nature and Destiny of Man: A Christian Interpretation*, vol. 1 (New York: Charles Scribner's Sons, 1941), 16.

Pneumatology

> *Why are you downcast, my soul;*
> *Why do you groan within me?*
> > Ps. 42: 6 *NAB*

Ruach is a powerful word. In Hebrew it connotes the breath of God. One who listens closely hears not an incomplete sigh of longing, but rather a sigh of fulfillment. The origin of the human sigh described in the first section makes audible the need to take in God's breath in order to survive. As Psalm 104: 29 avers: 'If you hide your face, they are dismayed; if you take away their breath, they perish.' The Spirit's presence through all of creation provides grounding for the sacramental imagination. The optimistic view of this theology rises not from nature itself, but is based upon God's breath sustaining creation and simultaneously moving the world and human beings to transcend themselves in concrete action.

There are numerous scriptural examples of the Spirit's breath.[11] The book of Genesis describes the work of the Spirit as the breath of God that brought order to chaos. The prophets, provoked by God's spirit, spoke a just word to the sinful monarchy when they brought disorder and injustice upon the dignity of God's creation. Those gifted with the presence of the Spirit received right judgment and expressed the will of God to the confused.[12] The prophet Isaiah reminds the people of Israel that God works through the anointed one to restore the fallen house of Israel.

The multiform work of the Spirit is a corrective to any overly optimistic theology based exclusively on theological anthropology. My own operative theology begins with anthropology or human experience but cannot stop there. Reflection on the work of the Spirit provides a dynamic that allows for a sacramental or positive interpretation of creation, precisely because the Spirit is at work in continuing re-creation. This re-creation or restoration does not imply that the created or material world is somehow the antithesis of the spiritual world as speculated by Greek dualism. Rather, the opposite of the spiritual is not created matter, but sin.[13] The Holy Spirit, at work in the anointed believer, transforms and enhances creation touched by sin. This perspective accounts for the dialogical perspective on human sinfulness while maintaining the anthropological starting point.

---

[11] Yves Congar's work, *I Believe in the Holy Spirit,* 3 vols. (New York: Seabury, 1983), provides exhaustive development to these propositions.

[12] Mic. 3: 8-9 *NAB*.

[13] *Cf.* Rom. 8.

Anointing or selection intimately ties the work of the Spirit to anthropology, not in an arrogant sense of divinization of the human in relation to the rest of creation, but as another means of God's sacramental presence revealed in creation. As Jesus dies on the cross, he 'hands over the spirit'.[14] The spirit of the anointed one is eschatologically now beyond incarnational focus and is once again the breath of God in, through, and beyond creation. Douglas John Hall categorizes this divine presence with the Hebrew word *Emmanuel,* God-with-us.[15] The term captures the Christian understanding of relationality.

Though often confused and esoteric, the relationship between Christians and their God through the Holy Spirit has sought definition in the concept of the Trinity. I am not as quick as Hall to dismiss this 'Athenian' concept because of my belief in the power and presence of the Holy Spirit. The relational character of the Spirit is the object of creation's groaning (sighing?) mentioned in Romans 8. The following quotation provides clearer voice to this theory:

> God is the triune God, the God of relationality, of overflowing goodness and graciousness; the disciple is a member of the body of Christ, incorporated into a cosmic communion whose animating principle is God's Holy Spirit. Christian existence manifests, therefore, a Trinitarian structure: it moves in the Spirit through Christ to the God who will be "everything to Everyone." (1 Cor. 5: 28 *NAB*)[16]

The tension provided between the 'anointed' of the charismatic church, which is to say those initiated into the community of disciples, and the 'institutional' church provides another corrective to a lofty theology. No baptized, confirmed, or anointed disciple is exempt from the responsibilities that accompany the gifts of the Spirit. Such corrective was provided in the first chapter of the *Dogmatic Constitution on the Church* (*Lumen Gentium*), in which the Second Vatican Council explains that in the mystery of the Church it is the action of the Triune God that is primary and not the earthly institution.[17] One notices the dialectical imagination at work even in the heart of sacramental territory!

---

[14] John 19: 30 *NAB*.

[15] Hall, 149-55.

[16] Joseph A. Komonchak, Mary Collins, and Dermot A. Lane, eds., *The New Dictionary of Theology* (Collegeville, MN: Liturgical, 1987), 483.

[17] Austin Flannery, OP, ed., *Vatican Council II: The Conciliar and Post Conciliar Documents* (Collegeville, MN: Liturgical, 1984), 350-58.

The longing of our hearts originates with the creative, prophetic, critical, restorative work of the Spirit guiding the body of Christ as a pilgrim church in this time and place. This work of the Holy Spirit points to Christ.

Christology

> *I will put an end to all sighing.*
> Isa. 21: 2 *NAB*

Jesus of Nazareth is the anointed one, relationally one with God and all of creation as *Emmanuel.* The basis of pneumatology is this promise that God is with us, yet remains the object of our future longing. The identity of who Jesus is, as the itinerant preacher from Nazareth or the cosmic Lord of the Universe, has been approached and will continue to be by Christian scholars. The list of Jesus' titles alone points to the endless potential of considering his identity: Emmanuel, Lord, Son of Man, Son of God, Logos, Wisdom, Word, Messiah, Prophet, Son of David, among others. For this reason, I leave the identity to the 'clearing in the middle'[18] by which the Council of Chalcedon (451), in a sort of *via negativa*, states that Jesus is fully God and fully human— the hypostatic union. My purpose here is to enunciate the operative theology that represents the horizon of my preaching. To that end, concentration will be made on what Jesus has done and how that influences the lives of the hearers of the Word. Though an imperfect categorization, the following represents a *functional* Christology. The source of these considerations is practical and liturgical: The Easter Triduum, which celebrates Jesus' life, death, and resurrection. The identity of Jesus is clearly implied though the following tripartite christological consideration.

Incarnation. 'And the Word became flesh and made his dwelling among us.'[19] The incarnation as a theological concept is central to Christianity and to the anthropological starting point of this paper. God's participation in creation as historical is a distinctive feature of the Christian faith that necessitates consideration of the importance of the sacramental imagination. God enfleshed becomes for us a 'classic' in the terminology of David Tracy.[20] Classics are universally recognized expressions of the human spirit that 'so disclose a

---

[18] The term is Douglas John Hall's.
[19] John 1: 14 *NAB.*
[20] David Tracy, *The Analogical Imagination: Christian Theology and the Culture of Pluralism* (New York: Crossroad, 1989), 99 *ff.*

compelling truth about our lives that we cannot deny them some kind of normative status.'[21] The incarnation provides us with a normative example of the fullness of humanity, of what it truly means to be the *imago dei*. Jesus of Nazareth as the normative human challenges us both in our consideration of who God is and who we are as the image of God.

God's identity expressed in the incarnation is Emmanuel—God with us. The incarnation provides a corrective to any theology that would make God's transcendence beyond our comprehension or our own humanity so sinful that God's love for us is not possible. The incarnation makes visible our relationship with God and how that relationship is lived. One needs to consider the activities of Christ in order to see how God is with us. Jesus called all people to holiness; no one was exempt from his portrayal of humanity as dignified. This dignified cohort included tax collectors, prostitutes, the poor and marginalized, even those wrapped in the royal cloth of just leadership and power. Jesus answered the sighs of humanity by pointing to the Father and the fullness of the Kingdom of God as the fulfillment a human longing that is fundamentally relational.

Jesus as the fullness of divinity provides a like corrective to an overly sacramental perspective regarding anthropology. Jesus dignified and redeemed creation through his life, death, and resurrection. His incarnation implies the necessity of redemption! That God took on flesh suggests that humanity, indeed all of creation, had a lost sense of potential and was overly concerned with power, possessions, and prestige. In this sense, the anthropological starting point is limited unless it is held up against the image of Jesus as the human being fully alive. Rahner claims that the incarnation is 'a presentation whereby men are mystagogically initiated into a recognition of their guilt situation'.[22] Such a dialectical regard for the fullness of life includes the incongruity of suffering as part of the human story.

Crucifixion. Jesus' life points to a God who does not hesitate to enter into the experience of suffering. As Jesus set his face toward Jerusalem, it seems that he understood suffering as his call and the primary focus of his mission. The human sigh results from two major anxieties: finiteness and death. Jesus confronts them both. Our belief is that he has defeated death by entering into the experience. A realistic theology recognizes that suffering remains. Was his mission to alleviate suffering or to somehow dignify it? Johann Baptist Metz claims this question must be faced: 'Theology, as I understand it, is first

---

[21] *Ibid.*, 108.
[22] Karl Rahner, 'Salvation', in *Sacramentum Mundi*, I (London: Herder and Herder, 1970), 405.

and foremost a theology sensitive to suffering.'[23] We claim that Jesus' passion is redemptive, even as we struggle to understand how suffering continues to exist. Even if all our political problems were solved, pain, sorrow, melancholy, and death would remain. What exactly did the Christ accomplish?

There are numerous soteriological theories, including deliverance, satisfaction, and demonstration.[24] In a simple summation of these theories: Jesus came to deliver us from our sins; was offered for us as some kind of a propitiatory lamb; or came to show us exactly how we should live if we hope to be saved. If the will of God is believed infinite, all of these theories lack, as they attempt to stretch human language to beyond the constraints of the finite. As Karl Rahner put it, 'These alternatives are too clumsy and simple to begin with.'[25] Rahner continues by asserting a two-fold, albeit limited, understanding of what Jesus has done:

> For, in the first place, by freely accepting the fate of death Jesus surrenders himself precisely to the unforeseen and incalculable possibilities of his existence; and, secondly, Jesus maintains in death his unique claim of an identity between his message and his person in the hope that in this death he will be vindicated by God with regard to his claim.[26]

It appears that Jesus threw himself into the mystery of uncontrolled suffering, even uttering his own sigh at the time of his death, in the sure hope that the suffering was somehow transformed in the will of the Father.

This event of personal suffering was not only a redemption of Jesus' own suffering in a given time and place, but of all suffering. It is no accident that our creed claims that Jesus 'descended into the dead' after the crucifixion. He cosmically enters into all historical suffering and thereby provides a meaning for that suffering which is beyond description. The event is redemptive for us in that we are obliged to respond through memory, narrative, and solidarity.[27] If we are to take the triune God seriously, we must remember not only the ineffable accomplishments of the deity, but also how those events relate to the good and evil events of all human history. The stories of brutality and sin must be told, especially those of the powerless in the past, present, and future.

---

[23] Johann Baptist Metz and Jürgen Moltmann, *Faith and the Future: Essays on Theology, Solidarity and Modernity* (New York: Maryknoll, 1995), viii.

[24] Hall, chapter seven, elucidates all these theories in great detail.

[25] Karl Rahner, *Foundations of Christian Faith* (New York: Crossroad, 1986), 255.

[26] *Ibid.*

[27] These thoughts are taken from Johann Baptist Metz, *Faith in History and Society: Towards a Practical Fundamental Theology*, trans., David Smith (New York: Crossroad, 1980), Part III.

These 'dangerous memories' and their recounting give expression to the depth of our sighs and force us into the 'solidarity of historical existence'[28]—leading to praxis, not only in the Christ event, but also in the political theologies of all disciples. The scandalous, suffering love of Christ saves us. This soteriological summation of the cross is highly optimistic, would even be Pelagian, were it not for its apocalyptic influence. The salvation won by Christ is only complete in the resurrection of the body.

Resurrection. The story of the Gospels does not end in the crucifixion. Nor is it tightly packaged in a clean conclusion by the resurrection. The entire narrative, though dangerous, is also proleptic. It is difficult to celebrate Good Friday without casting a glance that is at least cursory to Easter Sunday and the empty tomb. This part of the sigh is the most difficult to enunciate because it is rooted in a future made real only by faith. Our evaluation of the resurrection is based upon a question: Do we believe that Jesus of Nazareth, even the Christ of the cosmos, is authentic? The ending will not be known until all the living and the dead are touched by the story. At this point in history the ending is hardly neat. I believe in the empty tomb and the bodily resurrection of all the redeemed. I do not dare to bring the implications of that belief to neat conclusion here or in the operative theology of a funeral homily. I offer three warnings provided by Metz.[29]

The salvific event of the resurrection cannot be left on the level of historicity rather than that of the fullness of history. It cannot be considered only by one subject or culture in a limited situation, because it transcends both. In other words, the Christ event is not only about me and my culture, but regards all people of all times. In the words of John Macquarrie, ' … not the hope of the individual that he might be saved, out of this naughty world, but a hope for the world itself.'[30] Secondly, the event becomes more dangerous if only considered eschatologically as something in the future. Such an understanding would limit the action of a church that knows the messiah has come and that the people of God have an obligation to live as disciples now. Finally, that the idea of a 'suffering God' has taken upon himself all of the suffering of humanity and healed it is not realistic when contemporary suffering is acknowledged.

We are redeemed and remain disciples called to live and proclaim the message first proclaimed by the savior. As a preacher, this requires an explicit understanding of a practical or operative theology.

---

[28] *Ibid.*, 129.
[29] *Ibid.*, 131-32.
[30] John Macquarrie, *Thinking About God* (New York: Harper and Row, 1975), 225.

A Theology of Preaching

> *... our years end like a sigh.*
> Ps. 90: 9 *NAB*

Early in the twentieth century, Friedrich von Hügel described religion as a complex interactivity between three modalities: the institutional, the intellectual, and the mystical.[31] These modalities vaguely parallel the three religiously relevant aspects of experience in the theological reflection model of James Whitehead and Evelyn Eaton Whitehead: the experience of Christian tradition, personal and communal experience, and the experience of cultural systems.[32] No theology is developed in a vacuum. These distinctions will help me to define my own operative theology, based on the influences encountered to this point in my life.

The Institutional. As the tail end of the baby boom generation, I was coddled and grew up naturally optimistic. This optimism points to my natural affinity with a theologian of the sacramental imagination, Karl Rahner. Though my childhood was spent in the angst riddled days of the Cold War, I wanted for nothing. My family was lower middle class, which meant that I had shelter, food, and clothes—albeit hand-me-downs. My family was intact, influenced by minimal dysfunction. My longings were more spiritual and emotional than physical and survivalist. This optimism, influenced by my personal history, was given a name as I followed a vocational call to the Roman Catholic priesthood. My love for God deepened as I read sacramental theologians, including Rahner and John Courtney Murray; learned to pray in the tradition of Ignatius Loyola, finding God in all things; and was heavily influenced by the literature of Flannery O'Connor and Walker Percy.

My unrealistic optimism has diminished as I have deepened my appreciation of sin over the years. I attribute this to what I call the destruction of pillars of virtue. Among the reasons for my vocational choice were the priestly role models of a younger time. Recently, through a variety of means, I have discovered that among these role models there are molesters, alcoholics, pornography addicts, active homosexuals, and garden-variety sinners. Mixed into the shards of these tumbled models are my own vices and sins that have caused others pain—a difficult admission. My priesthood has compelled me

---

[31] Friedrich von Hügel, *The Mystical Element of Religion: As Studied in St Catherine of Genoa and Her Friends* (New York: Crossroad, 1999), 50–82.

[32] James D Whitehead and Evelyn Eaton Whitehead, *Method in Ministry: Theological Reflection and Christian Ministry,* Rev. Ed. (Kansas City: Sheed and Ward, 1995).

to face suffering in my own life and those I have served. The sheer passage of years has forced temperance upon unrealistic optimism. I am also less naïve about the presence of evil in historical, political, and social systems, including my own faith tradition. I am no less hopeful of God's dominion, only more realistic about the capacity of all people and groups or systems to sin and serve evil rather than good.

The Intellectual. The above experiences hardly compare to those of Johann Baptist Metz, whom I find most influential at this stage in my intellectual development. Metz, too, began his theological project with an anthropological starting point, based on the influence of his mentor, Karl Rahner. Metz quickly became dissatisfied with an anthropology that was exclusively philosophical; the social and political must also be accounted for. Metz had witnessed firsthand the capacity of social and political sin as a young soldier in Adolf Hitler's army. Sent on a mission, he returned to find his entire regiment wiped out. That memory had to be included in his theology if it was to be real. Metz wondered, 'What would happen if one took this sort of remembrance not to the psychologist, but into the Church? And if one did not allow oneself to be talked out of such unreconciled memories even by theology … ?'[33] For Metz, understanding the human subject is not simply a matter of some Kantian or Cartesian derivative of philosophical reflection; it must also take into account solidarity with the downtrodden and the narration of 'dangerous memories'.[34] A responsible theology must account for injustice and suffering, not only in the experience of the individual, but throughout the narratives of history and in the midst of all political experience, not only that of the imperium. Such honest reflection is dangerous as it is naturally subversive. The most dangerous memory of all is the passion of Jesus Christ. Rather than finding God in all things, one recognizes that God is most intensely found in *memoria passionis*.

Metz is attractive as a theological influence because his theology is political and addresses suffering through his concept of 'dangerous memories'. This approach provides a dialectic temper to the aforementioned optimism of a theology influenced by the sacramental imagination. Other theologians have helped me in the search for a hinge that offers a connection to these necessary theological foundations, namely Paul Tillich and Edward Schillebeeckx. There is a clearer resonance with Metz in that he allows for the anthropological starting point, while recognizing the aching nature of the

---

[33] Johann Baptist Metz, *A Passion for God: The Mystical-Political Dimension of Christianity*, ed. and trans. J Matthew Ashley (New York: Paulist, 1998), 2.

[34] Metz, *Faith in History and Society*.

existential sigh. Metz is also a theologian who deals frankly and clearly with the issue of theodicy, which must be faced honestly in order to develop a realistic theology.

The Mystical. Theology is not lived in an abstract arena, but in *praxis*, on the level of practical application within a given cultural situation. The metaphorical sigh that imbues this essay stands in a clearing surrounded by confusing eschatological thought. On the one hand is the hope of a world challenged by a theology of justice that recognizes the authority of those who suffer, as in the liberationist conclusions of Metz' thought. Alternately, there exists the groaning of the dialectical imagination that claims that this world is so destroyed by sin that its hope rests only in God, the Lord of time and space. I have found that my understanding of God has deepened in direct relation, not only to my life of prayer, but also to direct contact with suffering and oppression. It might be in the individual longing of my own heart—real enough—or in the direct encounter with the cross that I experience when baptism is taken seriously and hands are dirtied in acts clearly motivated by justice. The realm of experience merges the historical and intellectual, often through insights that convert.

An example helps to clarify this thought. I have no desire to be a rich man. This was not always the case. In fact, early in my life I believed material satisfaction would slake the thirst of my heart. That money was not the answer became clear to me when I was in college. I was culturally conditioned to seek fame through fortune and looked forward to a career in law and politics. Something was missing. It was not until I began to explore my spiritual side and the significance of the Gospel in my life that I understood that the American dream was not mine. My historical development and ensuing thoughts of success, conditioned by culture, came into question through intellectual development, but I was not converted until I had experienced the emptiness of the American dream. My claim is not that I have become a saintly lover of poverty, but that I find no fulfillment in getting ahead if it means leaving others behind.

That moment of conversion, a lived experience, remains for me a dangerous memory. It was a watershed in the narrative that led to my vocational choice and continues to form me as daily I discern God's will and the requisite reaction to the discovery of that will. This theological method of history, intellect and experience is dynamic and evolving, albeit not in a linear fashion. My own understanding, historically conditioned, is regularly challenged as I become more intellectually aware. As that awareness is lived and reflected upon in the day to day, I recognize my own limitations and sinfulness and that the fulfillment of my own longing for holiness and creation's groaning for completeness, points to the fullness of the Reign of God. It is a theology that allows neither the indifference of individualism nor the idealism of the possibility of creating a utopia. This operative theology influences my understanding of preaching.

Conclusion

Time has taught me the importance of imagination when it comes to the 'art and craft' of preaching. It is in the craft (after prayer, exegesis, and theological reflection) that I am apt to use a variety of metaphors, images, and narrative in my preaching. I believe preaching is an act of the imagination. The process of preparing a homily normally provides me some kind of a spiritual spark, which leads to an idea, followed by an image that opens the idea to the world of multi-valent interpretation. That interpretation is the intersection of the respective imaginations of the preacher and hearer of the Word. That is the reason for the anthropological starting point for my operative theology of preaching. The intersection is often a place of surprise. The initial spark or idea, with which I was inspired, is not always the same idea with which the listener is inspired. I can think of no greater evidence of the Spirit at work in the Church today! Even a bad homily can provide inspiration for some listeners, whose hunger for the Word overcomes the limitation of the prophet. The longing heart of the preacher is not identical to that of the hearer, though a good homily can bring them to a level of convergence.

The Word of God is alive. The Holy Spirit of God, as promised, dwells in our midst. I am not convinced that the Word is always experienced as living. When I teach homiletics to permanent deacon candidates, I talk about the passion of the preacher and how that passion is often lacking in homilies that I hear. One wonders if the proclaimers have ever encountered the power of the Spirit in their own story; if they have ever been threatened by a dangerous memory; if they have placed their hands in the passionate wounds of Christ. I believe that prayer is the source of that passion. By prayer, I mean living in regular conversation with God, as encountered in our experiences.

The passion, inspired by the Spirit, needs to be sustained through individual and communal responsibility. Through theological reflection the preacher ought to listen for the voice of the Spirit in the community and the world. The entire community has received the breath of God and has been called to discipleship. The result is a responsibility on the part of the preacher to constantly learn and improve the art and craft of preaching. The community, too, is responsible for this improvement of preaching, through honest evaluation of the homily and through securing for the preacher time for study, reflection, and continuing formation.

This communal responsibility leads to a sense of intimacy akin to Jesus and his closest friends who often heard him preach. This intimate tie affords the possibility for a living word, a community of love, and a proper understanding of Emmanuel. My vision for preaching requires this sense of love. I would like to think that at a time of separation or death of the preacher, there would be copious tears, knowing that something was lost.

Reflecting on his thoughts at the death of his mentor, Metz recalls the words he wrote on the occasion of Rahner's death in 1984. As a conclusion, these words capture beautifully the essence of my own theological experience:

> Karl Rahner has never interpreted Christianity as the happy conscience of an advanced bourgeois condition that has been purged of every endangered hope, every vulnerable and stubborn longing … . Through it all there remained in him a longing, which I never felt to be sentimental, nor something that stormed the heavens, but which was much more a hushed *sigh* of the creature, like a wordless cry for light before the face of God shrouded in darkness.[35]

---

[35] Metz, *A Passion for God*, 5. Emphasis added.

FIND THE COMMON GROUND
Audrey Borschel

As in much music from the eighteenth century, when balanced musical phrases were organized in two parts referred to as the antecedent and the consequent, I sometimes conduct my own theological dialogue in contrasting phrases with the sacramental and dialectical imaginations. The first part of the phrase is contentedly sacramental, while the second dialectically rebuts what I said in the first. The sacramental protagonist plays a ground bass, a steady pattern, an ostinato mantra of conjunct intervals played continuously, while the dialectical antagonist is represented by disjunct, dissonant music playing screeching intermittent appositional lines above the bass. Although I typically conceptualize God in terms of the sacramental imagination, struggles and conflicts infiltrate that comfortable vision, replacing certitude with the angst of less ethereal realities, such as the perceived distance of God, the poor judgments of ecclesial or political leaders. At times I hear the sacramental and dialectical separately, but as distinct threads sounding concurrently. For example, I love the Church when it manifests itself as a sacramental community, but I also experience church as an institution capable of creating obstacles to community. And so, I find myself doing theology from both the sacramental and dialectical perspectives in these ways: often at the same time, separately, overlapping, and trying to find balance between the two poles.[1]

Within this personalized conception of the tensions within the sacramental and dialectical framework, I envision a preaching ministry that nourishes and supports the faith of the people of God. I feel that preaching should enflame the hearts of listeners, prompting them to embrace Christian discipleship more fully and intensely through charity and service. Just as a complicated symphonic work evokes diverse responses from listeners, so preaching that is conceived and prepared with the plurality of the listeners'

---

[1] Mary Catherine Hilkert, *Naming Grace: Preaching and the Sacramental Imagination* (New York: Continuum, 1997), 19–43.

experiences in mind evokes a range of desirable responses. The preacher needs to include everyone in the assembly, reaching out to the people in different ways: restoring hope to those who struggle with their faith, challenging listeners to live more justly, or providing encouragement when dealing with daunting issues. Without ever hearing the terms sacramental and dialectical, members of the assembly will dialogue with their contrasting perceptions and feelings regarding the presence and distance of God, grace and sin, the 'already' and the 'not-yet' of the Reign of God.

God in the sacramentality of creation

The ground of my operative theology of preaching, as well as the *ēthos* I hope I project as a preacher, is a sacramentally-imagined theological theme, 'God is love, and whoever remains in love remains in God and God in him.'[2] This also formed the basis for Karl Rahner's theological reflections.[3] In my theological vision, dialectical and sacramental characteristics are woven throughout a set of variations that embellish this theme of love, contributing incarnational, christological, inclusive, feminist, ecumenical, Benedictine, and eucharistic understandings to my holistic theology, which is based on relationship with God, with all of creation, and our engagement with the person and ministry of Jesus of Nazareth, the Christ.

My preaching is conditioned in part by my contemplative experience of God in the sacramentality of creation, time, and encounter, tinged at times, by the awareness of dialectical aspects entering into that experience. For example, God is present to me in the breath-taking palette of autumn leaves, in my blessed marriage, in the holy time of meals and conversation with close friends, in the quiet time I spend in prayer and reflection, in the music that touches my heart, in the affirmations of parishioners, in the sacraments that I receive and in which I assist, in the stillness of right now, in my weakness, in my discouragement, in my frustration, in my surrender, in my vulnerability, in the 'I love you, Lord' that erupts out of me at times throughout the day, in my grieving, in my fear and anxiety, in the *kairos* moments when I admit my failures and sinfulness, in unexpected grace-filled encounters, during the ordinary tasks of ministry, in the faith of all who remain Roman Catholic, despite their anger and disappointment with the Church, in new life and in the recreated life of those who have lost loved ones, in the work of women theologians and ministry models who complement previous understandings

---

[2]   1 John 4: 16b *NAB*.
[3]   Hilkert, 31-34.

of God, and in the intensity of being with the disenfranchised, disadvantaged, and poor in spirit.

These raw materials of lived experience and encounter with divine mystery influence how and what I preach. The dialectical infiltrates a basically sacramental rhythm when my consciousness is raised over injustices that contradict all that Jesus taught. Because of this, I preach counterculturally, to promote concepts of seeking, becoming aware of, and remaining in God's presence, the value of keeping sabbath, exploring a contemplative vision for the world, and nurturing all relationships. I hope to offset some of those negative forces, which, like intermittent screeching interpolations of piercing piccolos and E flat clarinets in the symphony, challenge the peace and harmony of the comforting pattern of the ground bass.

I believe and preach that God is the source of all our being, the God-with-us, our Emmanuel who loves us unconditionally, our God who reveals the holy through relationship with us and through our interactions with one another. People who become aware of God's love for them and are drawn by that experience of love toward its source become love themselves, capable of revealing God's love to others. I try to help people realize that our creator God wants to accompany us through each movement of our lives, the passages of exultant joy and sacred profundity, through struggle, and in the final journey toward divine union. This union, ideally the mutual desire of both God and human, derives from God's covenant, the self-giving promise of *being with* and *being for* the people, the *ground base* of a permanent relationship between God and people.

God's being-with

Our parishioners need to know that God seeks our participation in the enterprise of salvation, calling 'for friends, for covenant partners, for laborers in the vineyard, for stewards'.[4] And yet, as Karl Barth said, our relational God is 'wholly other',[5] but oriented to creation:

> I deliver all who cling to me,
> raise the ones who know my name,
> answer those who call me,
> stand with those in trouble.[6]

---

[4] Douglas John Hall, *Professing the Faith: Christian Theology in a North American Context* (Minneapolis: Fortress, 1993), 103.

[5] *Ibid.*, 148.

[6] Ps. 91: 14-15 *ICEL*.

As a Benedictine oblate, I draw from the anthropology and theology of the psalms and readings of the Liturgy of the Hours, as well as from the *Rule of St Benedict*. Instructions pertaining to relationships between God and neighbor permeate the chapters of the *Rule*. These directives transfer well to the parish community. I have preached about our need for openness and attentive listening to God and to each other, which comes from understanding the promise of obedience to the will of God. Benedictines also promise stability of heart, which asks us to remain committed Christians through our personal responsibility and tenacity, to deepen our relationship with God, as well as with colleagues and loved ones, and to serve our vocational call with dedication and purpose. Faithfulness to the spirit of monastic life, the third promise for the oblate, includes making prayer a priority, becoming rooted in and preferring nothing to Christ, and encouraging the building of community in different ways and with diverse groups of people. These values are key to evangelization and to increasing commitment to participation in the mission of the Church.[7] As a pastoral theologian, I apply theology to pastoral situations instead of speaking about theological concepts in the abstract. Douglas John Hall agrees that we must not isolate God from God's relationship to the world: 'God's being is already God's being-with.'[8] The relationship between God and a receptive human being is the prototype of the sacred relationship we admire between a husband and wife in a happy marriage. Both the bond between God and the person, as well as the bond between two people whom God has joined, symbolize stability in creation. Witnessing successful relationships, such as the strong faith of an individual or a marriage that is obviously life-giving, encourages others to become open to God's presence. The already-begun Reign of God that we occasionally glimpse becomes animated by loving relationships of companions on the journey, oriented toward our self-communicating God, who communicates 'being-there, being-with, and being-for the creature'.[9] In other words, God is what God is communicating: God is love.

St Paul wrote to Timothy: 'Everything God created is good; nothing is to be rejected when it is received with thanksgiving, for it is made holy by the invocation of God in prayer.'[10] I believe that all of us who are created in the image of God are responsible for the prudent use and stewardship of the earth's resources; we must use our freedom to make wise choices, especially since we know our decisions potentially impact all of creation.[11] I preach an

---

[7] St Benedict, *The Rule of St Benedict in English*, ed. Timothy Fry, OSB (Collegeville, MN: Liturgical, 1982), chapters 1, 4, 5, 53, 72.

[8] Hall, 73.

[9] *Ibid.*, 147.

[10] 1 Tim. 4: 4-5 *NAB*.

[11] *Catechism of the Catholic Church*, #2415.

incarnational theology affirming that God offers grace in the midst of the goodness of creation, as well as in our suffering. However, we ignore God's offer of grace when we reveal our self-centeredness and selfishness, each inherent in our shadow side. We distance ourselves from God and from people through sinful acts and by ignoring the needs of others. Mistaking ourselves for God, we capably destroy creation's beauty and abundance, as well as life-sustaining relationships. We destroy the unity that God intends for all of creation: 'The web of life is one. Our mistreatment of the material world diminishes our own dignity and sacredness, not only because we are destroying resources that future generations of humans need, but because we are engaging in actions that contradict what it means to be human.'[12]

Attracted to temptations that encourage us to ignore Jesus Christ, our way, truth, and life, we engage in destructive behaviors resulting from our desire for power and acquisition. As preachers, we can help people prepare to hear the power of God's voice in those scriptures that urge us to resist immoral and unethical behaviors and to remain focused on the teachings of Jesus. Our preaching should empower people to recognize their weaknesses, take ownership of their sins and addictions, and seek courage to find their own healing. Our preaching and pastoral care in combination should provide spiritual support to deal with struggles and help people continue on their journey of faith in community.

Jesus the enfleshment of God

God chose to communicate with us through the humanity of Jesus. The Jesus with whom I identify my life and ministry was fully human, passionate, relational, and totally self-giving. Jesus, the enfleshment of God, offered a unique path toward holiness, providing remediation to a religious society that needed transforming. I admire the simplicity and humility with which he presented his messages of love and the preferential option for the poor, but I hear a dialectical voice that decries how this message has been diluted and filtered over centuries of political and ecclesial accretions and detours from the path.

The Jesus who speaks to me from the Gospels and who preaches to my community is a risk-taking dissenter, neither passive nor *nice* much of the time. If I preach this Word who speaks to my heart, I must reflect his passionate, countercultural, and radical character. When Jesus identified and

---

[12] 'Renewing the Earth', in 'Care for the Earth' (Indianapolis: Indiana Catholic Conference, 2000): 2.

preached against injustice, he irritated complacent and advantaged people. Our culture today continues to resist revising attitudes and policies that would favor the poor and oppressed. The *not-yet* illusiveness of the Reign of God prods me to preach against complacency and for our ongoing conversion. But how far can we take this, or, as Walter Burghardt asks, 'How concrete dare I get?'[13] He concludes: 'Each issue calls for discernment; some call for blood, sweat, and tears.'[14] I would add that negative responses to such preaching do result in post-preaching blood, sweat, and tears!

Being human, we resist sacrifices or discomforts of any kind. However, it was only through Jesus' embrace of suffering, his emptying himself for all of humanity on the cross, that he accomplished his mission. If we refuse to identify with the cross of Jesus, we reject his message. Through the cross, which reveals, absorbs, and projects all the worst depravities, we still discover God's powerful companionship and grace to move us out of chaos into new, resurrected life. In our own self-emptying at the cross we learn to surrender and grow.

Hagiographies provide exquisite models for preaching about the cross. The saints experienced purification, but only by dying to themselves through their sacrificial work. The lesson I need to keep reinforcing for myself is that saints choose to live *within* struggle and not run from it. They suffer in order to eliminate the sources of pain, enabling others to freely experience love: 'These are the ones who have survived the time of great distress; they have washed their robes and made them white in the blood of the Lamb.'[15] When we preach the cross, we empower our hearers to engage with the cross and to trust the basic premise of covenant that God is *with us* and *for us*, both in the struggle and in the ambiguity of its resolution:

> God assumes the cross in solidarity with and love for the crucified of history, with those who suffer the cross. God tells them, "Absurd as it is, the cross can be the pathway of a marvelous liberation. But you must take it up in freedom and love. Then you will deliver the cross from its absurdity, and yourself from yourself. ... For liberty and love are greater than all absurdities, and stronger than death. For you can make them, too, your road to me." ...The cross is not there to be understood. It is there to be taken up—to be carried in the footsteps of

---

[13] Walter Burghardt, SJ, *Preaching: The Art and the Craft* (New York: Paulist, 1987), 132.
[14] *Ibid.*, 134.
[15] Rev. 7: 14 *NAB*.

the Son of Man, who took up his cross and by that cross
accomplished our redemption.[16]

All theologies of liberation scorn the status quo and the passive
acceptance of evil. Among the oppressed, women have traditionally been
subjected to abuse. In light of the history and the current perpetuation of
physical and emotional suffering inflicted on women by men, a theology of
the cross that encourages the endurance of suffering, without trying to
transform those who perpetuate the suffering, is repugnant to most women.
In fact, 'The call to "take up the cross" works directly against their liberation.'[17]
While numerous theologians question God's desire for oppressed women
and other victims of society to remain scapegoats, other theologians place
more value on a theology of redemptive suffering. Among them is Kwok
Pui-lan, originally from Hong Kong, who writes on the relational dimension
of suffering. I find this focus on relationship especially compatible with how
I preach the cross, that we are, in fact, accompanied by Jesus: 'It is the very
person on the Cross that suffers like us, who was rendered as no-body that
illuminates the tragic human existence and speaks to countless women in
Asia. ... We see Jesus as the God who takes the human form and suffers and
weeps with us.'[18]

I preach out of a feminist theology that eschews violence. As
counterpoint to violence, I call for a process theology of peace, healing,
nurture, promoting the success of creation, assistance with its preservation,
and cooperation with redemption.[19] With some exceptions, men have always
dominated the decisions about waging war. War has rarely been described as
anti-Christian; more often it is glorified. For some reason, the absence of war,
which we call peace, receives little media attention.

Feminist theology and preaching seeks to persuade a male-centered
world system that women and men are equal and complementary images of
God. It is necessary to replace patriarchal images of violence, power, and
domination with new images of being in relation with God and with each
other. The Jesus of my prayer and preaching is the inclusive Jesus, who freed
us forever from the constraints of a theology of domination. If only everyone

---

[16] Leonardo Boff, *Passion of Christ, Passion of the World* (New York: Orbis, 1987), 116.

[17] John B Cobb Jr, in William A Beardslee *et al.*, *Biblical Preaching on the Death of Jesus* (Nashville: Abingdon, 1989), 133-34, quoted in André Resner Jr, *Preacher and Cross: Person and Message in Theology and Rhetoric* (Grand Rapids, MI/Cambridge, UK: William B Eerdmans, 1999), 143.

[18] Kwok Pui-lan, 'God Weeps with Our Pain,' *East Asia Journal of Theology* 2, no. 2 (1984): 220-32, quoted in Elisabeth Schüssler Fiorenza, *Jesus: Miriam's Child, Sophia's Prophet—Critical Issues in Feminist Theology* (New York: Continuum, 1995), 103.

[19] Hall, 166.

believed that. How ironic that human beings continue to enjoin violence and brutality to their causes, even and *especially* as they espouse the various religious traditions that are rooted in Abraham and Sarah.

Toward a more balanced theology

Feminine views of anthropology help mold a balanced theology. Such a balance has been missing until now, since the male point of view dominated everywhere and the complementary perspective that women bring to issues was largely suppressed. Balanced notions about creatureliness and God's will for us can occur only when men recognize that women have much to contribute to all of life's conversations. All people need to hear women preach and to become acquainted with the voices of women in Scripture.

Phyllis Trible's phrase, 'texts of terror', has raised my awareness of how lectionary readings affect the congregation.[20] Scripture excerpts are often misunderstood because they are taken out of their original context to serve a function in the lectionary, ostensibly to fit with the other readings. Parts of the passages that are omitted, either preceding or following the included segment, are often necessary for fuller understanding. The difficult New Testament texts that appear to exclude women and others, or seem to address important issues of conduct in absolutes, present challenges for preaching. How we preach on those texts, such as Mark 10: 2-16, an easily misunderstood passage, may determine whether some people choose to remain in the Church.

I believe that as we preach and lead prayer, we need to model inclusive language. Language can alienate or unite us as we express what we think and feel about God. In today's culture, using only the male pronoun to refer to God creates a barrier for many women, because what we speak and hear conditions our beliefs, as well as those of the next generation. Building on the work of Jürgen Moltmann, Elizabeth Johnson unpacks essentially gender-biased doctrine through the use of inclusive language. For example, as she discusses the persons of the Trinity, she begins with Father-Son-Spirit, but she concludes by transcending gender completely, helping to expand the understanding of relationship and function within the community of triune persons: '... the three interweave each other in various patterns of saving activity and can be spoken about in concepts such as giving over and receiving back, being obedient and being glorified, witnessing, filling, and actively glorifying.'[21]

---

[20] Hilkert, 72.

[21] Elizabeth A Johnson, *She Who Is: the Mystery of God in Feminist Theological Discourse* (New York: Crossroad, 1996), 195.

From Gethsemene to resurrection to eucharist

As we travel with Jesus during his ministry through the liturgical year, Jesus matures as Good Shepherd, but he lives his final days revealing the paschal mystery as Jesus, Lamb of God. I am comfortable preaching about Jesus' experiences from Gethsemane to resurrection, because I identify my experiences of loss and healing with the paschal mystery. Retaining hope that the spirit of the risen Christ is alive in the world and will transform the lives of those who mourn, we are called as preachers to address the stages of emptiness, grief, anticipation, and longing for new life in those to whom we minister. Jesus' community of disciples had to mourn, heal, and begin to understand that even in death, Jesus was still present, but changed. My preached theology of resurrection contains hope, that even in the bleakest moments, life will be re-created and renewed out of our suffering—a new song will be sung.

During the first season of healing following the death of my son Nick in 1995, my parish community nurtured my call to ministry through its ministry to me. Shortly after Nick died, I wrote a song that reflected my understanding of a theology of Christian community:

> Will you meet me in the Garden, will you join me on my knees?
> Will you stay with me for a little while, will you listen to my needs?
> Will you help me gather strength and hope to go on through all my pain?
> Will you meet me in the Garden, until I'm whole again?
>
> Will you share your wealth of faith with me and encourage me to grow?
> Will you challenge me to seek the truth, will you teach me all you know?
> Will you see to it I live the Word in the fullest sense of live,
> Will you urge me to go out and give in the fullest sense of give?
>
> Will you lead me from the Garden, will you guide me on my way?
> Will you care for me as I leave this world, will you pray for me that day?
> And should you call me to your Garden, I will always care for you.
> I will pray for you and love you, I will bring you comfort, too.

The community participated in the healing of me, their suffering sister, and led me to new life. Imitating Christ who modeled the behavior of *being with* and *being for* the human person, the people of the community responded out of their experience of Christ's healing spirit. Having received their support, I was moved to express my gratitude by reinvesting the charity received in the healing of others. The season of my cross then segued into a season of resurrection.

Hans Küng, in commenting on the resurrection of Jesus, distinguished between resurrection as an historical event and resurrection as an event of theological faith:

> The resurrection faith—a truly reasonable attitude of trust and hope—is directed to the reality and the efficacy of God himself, who in Jesus conquered death. Resurrection then is undoubtedly a happening of faith. ... Easter is primarily an event for Jesus himself. Jesus lives again *through God—as a challenge to faith*. ... The resurrection message is therefore a testimony of faith, not a product of faith.[22]

The Easter stories reveal that something powerful took place in the community of disciples that restored their faith and encouraged them to believe that Christ would always be present to them. They were changed, consoled, freed from the limitations that bound them as they moved toward new life. Our awareness of Christ's presence in our midst likewise heals and energizes us to become effective disciples. Lines from St Patrick's deeply theological poem, a favorite of mine since I was a child, beautifully describe that awareness of *being with* the resurrected Christ:

> Christ be with me, Christ within me,
> Christ behind me, Christ before me,
> Christ beside me, Christ to win me,
> Christ to comfort and restore me,
> Christ beneath me, Christ above me,
> Christ in quiet, Christ in danger,
> Christ in hearts of all that love me,
> Christ in mouth of friend and stranger.[23]

---

[22] Hans Küng, *Eternal Life?* (New York: Image, 1985), 106.

[23] From 'St Patrick's Breastplate', in *Saint Meinrad Prayerbook* (St Meinrad, IN: Abbey Press, 1995), 125.

Each time we celebrate Eucharist, we are obliged to renew our commitment to our own transformation and to that of the world. We take the raw materials of life and bless them, mindful of our brokenness and the fragile nature of the reconciliation and peace we are bound to further. Our participation requires that we become the sacrament we receive. Jesus' mission of loving the world into transformation is linked to how we welcome strangers, build trust, remove barriers, and provide opportunities for people of diverse backgrounds to grow in appreciation of each others' gifts.

One of the most contentious barriers to Christian unity is the table of the Lord. It is clear that Karl Rahner saw the potential of the Eucharist as uniting rather than dividing:

> … insofar as the Eucharist is the sacrament of the most radical and most real presence of the Lord in this celebration in the form of a meal, the Eucharist is also the fullest actualization of the essence of the church. For the church neither is nor wants to be anything else but the presence of Christ in time and space. And insofar as everyone participates in the same meal of Christ, who is the giver and gift at the same time, the Eucharist is also the sign, the manifestation and the most real actualization of the church insofar as the church is and makes manifest the ultimate unity of all men in the Spirit, a unity which has been founded by God in grace.[24]

When we are successful at being eucharistic people, Christ's spirit flows out from our altars as we move into the larger church beyond the brick walls. We need to apply a theology of ecumenism based on a loving respect for all traditions in order to encourage mutual growth, tolerance, and the prospect for unity. I have experienced this growth as a member of the Indiana Roman Catholic-Disciples of Christ dialogue team. In addition, the diversity within my family, neighborhood, and parish broadens my insights and helps me speak with confidence about the benefits of ecumenism and inter-religious dialogue. Contributions from all religious traditions help us to appreciate and to understand the pluralism of God's saving activity in the world.

We do not have to look beyond our parishes to see the need for ecumenism. Since many more Catholics are marrying non-Catholics, we have both opportunity and responsibility to preach ecumenism, as I did this past feast of All Saints, when I praised the contributions of several holy, non-

---

[24] Karl Rahner, *Foundations of Christian Faith: An Introduction to the Idea of Christianity* (New York: Crossroad, 1994), 427.

Catholic people. If we preach about what binds us together as people of faith, we could make non-Catholic spouses feel so welcome that they choose to join the community as full members. We should focus more of our pastoral attention on the needs of families practicing two religious traditions. As the number of non-Catholic parents increases, our preaching must be inclusive and hospitable to those who accompany their spouses and children to Catholic liturgy and sacramental preparation. Margaret O'Gara, author of *The Ecumenical Gift Exchange*, underscores Pope John Paul II's comment that the future of Christian unity is related to expressing sorrow for the injustices of our past.[25] We will need to be preachers of reconciliation in our quest for unity. An ecumenical, hospitable, preached ecclesiology of our common baptism at the parish will acknowledge to all present that diverse believers contribute desirable timbres to the richness of an orchestration scored for different voices, each praising God with the instrument God gave them.

Called to preach the Word of God in many different ways during worship, in pastoral care, faith formation, and action for justice, I will continue to seek truth and wisdom from God and the community as I preach the justice, love, and peace of the inclusive Jesus Christ. Ministering to the voices of dissent and the voices opposed to change, I seek to find the common ground, the sacramental imagination in the midst of the *detunings* of the dialectical imagination, which threaten our mission of living as Christian disciples who long to do God's will. As we commemorate the one hundredth anniversary of Aaron Copland's birth,[26] we can apply his comment about music to our preaching: 'We don't compose our music to make [people] comfortable, we create it to stir them up.'[27]

---

[25] Margaret O'Gara, *The Ecumenical Gift Exchange* (Collegeville, MN: Liturgical, 1998), 33.

[26] 15 November 2000.

[27] Aaron Copland, BBC interview, 1981, rebroadcast on National Public Radio, *Morning Edition*, 14 November 2000.

THE PULPIT IS A MOUNTAIN

Daniel Francis, CSsR

With no illusions of ever reaching the summit, a friend and I nevertheless started out on a trail that would eventually bring a more robust climber to the top of Mount Robson, the tallest peak in the Canadian Rockies. Although we had been told at the ranger station that clouds frequently shroud the top of the mountain, I was disappointed upon rounding a corner to have such a promising view blocked. I voiced my thoughts: 'Why keep climbing if the summit is obscured?' My friend's reaction was the opposite: 'The clouds playfully entice us to come closer.'

God both conceals and reveals—knowable, nevertheless unintelligible; captivating, yet beyond our grasp; inviting, but withdrawn. Potent and playful, God is the summit and the source of our desires.

It is difficult when speaking of our experience of God, God's expression, God's realm, to steer clear of a pervasive anthropocentrism with respect to the divine. My observations about God 'concealing and revealing' belie this tendency: God's self-communication does not by nature withhold or conceal; yet, on this side of our human limited awareness, this is often how it seems.

How graced we are by God's gift of Jesus: both Human One and God's Eternal Word. This word made flesh is the apex of God's conversation with creation. Jesus makes manifest the Realm of God in his words and deeds and especially in his entrusting of self to God at Gethsemane and Calvary. In this outpouring of self to God, reinforced by the message of his preaching and teaching, Jesus proclaims the Realm of God.

If an anthropology is designated Christian, it is so because it follows the pattern of Christ and his Spirit. Something radical happens in the life of the Christian disciple. Whether or not it is named or appreciated, as the Holy Spirit conforms the disciple to Christ, the disciple becomes a witness, being moved toward expression, toward a voicing of the story of his or her experience of the living Christ. Disciples as such are Witnesses to the Proclaimer of the

Realm. The disciple as witness proclaims Christ, God's Word.

While preaching and witnessing, the Church mounts Sinai again and again to learn and tell of God and what God is revealing in God's people. Bushes are ablaze on holy ground, whether we see them or not. Calling us by name, God has heard our groaning and invites us to trust in a promise of freedom, always still another exodus and a newer covenant. Preaching and witness attempt to wrap words around the mystery of these transforming encounters with the divine. Mary Catherine Hilkert calls us to become a partner in these encounters or conversations begun by God, employing the analogical language of 'sacramental imagination'. The preacher as witness invites people into the experience of the Realm of God by naming the mystery as they experience it and as they are intended by God to experience it in their daily lives. As Belden Lane understands, this naming of grace is ever elusive:

> The seductive, ambivalent landscape of the half-seen mountain—able to be read but *not* read, provoking as much confusion as it does insight—is a metaphor of the effort to speak of God. ... [C]loud-covered Sinai is where all graven images—all attempts to contain God's mystery (either in stone or in speech)—are ultimately declared inadequate.[1]

Sandra Schneiders understands that God's elusive self-revelation is meant to be gradual, respectful, and never overwhelming. It is an invitation to a shared life with God. The Word became flesh to 'speak to humanity in a language we could understand.'[2] Lane also speaks to this point:

> Looking upon God's act of masking or veiling as a means of protecting the divine majesty from prying human eyes, or as a way of protecting us from a grandeur too terrifying to perceive, we forget that God's hiding is rooted first of all in divine compassion. God hides not only to protect, but also to draw us to herself in love.[3]

Deus absconditus reveals *Deus ludens*. God's hide-and-seek serves as our 'entrance' into the divine realm. This divine invitation to mutuality requires intellectual and spiritual humility, a recognition that we do not know about

---

[1] Belden C Lane, *The Solace of Fierce Landscapes: Exploring Desert and Mountain Spirituality* (New York/Oxford: Oxford UP, 1998), 102.

[2] Sandra Schneiders, *Written That You May Believe: Encountering Jesus in the Fourth Gospel* (New York: Crossroad, 1999), 49.

[3] Lane, 179.

God so much as we know that God is with and for us (Martin Buber's 'I and Thou'; Douglas John Hall's *'pro nobis'*). Preaching is 'disclosure talk' (Martin Heidegger) unveiling the Realm of God, who is the ground of all our experience and yet nevertheless 'wholly other' (*'totaliter alliter'*, Rudolph Otto and Karl Barth).

We speak of our encounter with God with images: God who parts the seas, gives us water from the rock, and feeds us with quail; God who wrestles with us in the night and speaks to us in dreams. Ultimately, however, images do not bring us close enough to the incomprehensible mystery of God. God offers to 'empty himself' and to be embodied for us as Emmanuel.

The preacher as witness

In the self-emptying *kenosis* of his human incarnation, Jesus learned to listen (to obey) and to trust. We are told he grew in wisdom and grace, and a christology from below allows us to appreciate Jesus as being in 'in process'. Both before and during his public ministry, Jesus was molded by his culture and upbringing, his exposure to Romans and other foreign peoples, his experience of the Baptizer's movement, and his dealings with religious and civil leaders. As he was molded by his experience, nothing became more central to his sense of mission than proclaiming or preaching the Realm of God, even to the point of causing scandal and finally incurring a sentence of death.

The death of Jesus on the cross expresses his radical decision to trust God. Many others throughout history have died for causes, and many have endured torture. Jesus' suffering and death is supreme and salvific insofar as it was the definitive mark of consistency in his relationship with the Father. Once on the cross, he 'incarnates' the altar, the priest, and the lamb of sacrifice. The one who communicated through words and signs now preaches most eloquently without saying a word.

Jesus is the new Abraham and Isaac who climbs obediently the mountains of Gethsemane and Calvary, obscured as they were in clouds of confusion, pain, and ultimately betrayal and loneliness. The Father who once spoke from the cloud at his baptism and affirmed him at the transfiguration is now hidden and mute. Jesus was called to absolute trust in his relationship to God, with firm faith in God's will. Jesus demonstrates well 'the depth of divine love', but he is not a teacher at the cross. Perhaps, indeed, he becomes one, but only after the resurrection. At Calvary, he is student, son of a sorrowful mother and silent father, abandoned friend, misunderstood preacher, blasphemer, and hated zealot.

If Redemptorists such as myself claim to follow Christ the Redeemer, it is to proclaim the Realm of God through trust in the will of God: 'In Jesus, relationship with the Father and the realization of the [Realm] of God are brought together in unity.'[4] God's Realm is revealed in the words and miraculous deeds of Jesus. But Jesus was most eloquent in his proclamation of that realm when he trusted in his relationship to God to get him beyond Gethsemane and ultimately to Easter Sunday. The call to this eloquent proclamation has now been handed on to us who by the power of the Spirit experience the grace of belief in the resurrection. We as preachers are called to faithful proclamation, both in and out of the pulpit, a proclamation which most essentially points to Jesus himself and to the Realm of God.

Just as the fingers of God and humanity come close, but never touch, in Michelangelo's *Creation of Adam* on the ceiling of the Sistine Chapel, there is at the same time an intimacy and alienation in our relationship with God: an intimacy at the peak moments of our life (Abraham Maslow); an alienation that occurs through our refusal to climb the mountain of the Lord due to the obfuscation brought on by our own sinful propensity or inability. We fail at times, for a variety of reasons, to rise above the horizons of our own sin. For this reason it is important that the twin images of the garden and the cross be one symbol of ultimate contact (Jesus' powerful *fiat*) between heaven and earth of loving trust in God's will. From our founder, St Alphonsus Liguori, Redemptorists have inherited the legacy of telling of this contact.

Burdened by overwork, Father Alphonsus of the Liguori family in Naples was urged by friends to take a rest from the numerous ministries in which he was engaged as a young priest: visiting the prostitutes who were patients at the 'Hospital of the Incurables', setting up numerous night chapels to be run by laity, composing hymns, and many other activities. Shortly thereafter, when his boat was nearly overturned in a storm at sea, he was forced aground in a remote part of southern Italy. Alphonsus spent the rest of his so-called holiday evangelizing the poor goatherds in the small town in which found himself. In the course of this ministry, he discovered his true vocation: to organize a band of itinerant missionaries whose express goal would be to preach good news to the poor.

The motto of my Redemptorist congregation is: 'With God there is bountiful redemption.' This is a reference to Psalm 130, which begins with the cries of one sinking in the depths of despair due to personal sinfulness. As a Redemptorist preacher-witness, I am nudged gently but consistently to live the words I preach and preach the good news to the poor and most abandoned. In the context in which I normally minister, I identify these to

---

[4] 'Charism 2000: A Journey in Redemptorist Spirituality' (Rome, 2000), 9.

be people who are poor spiritually and abandoned pastorally. This preaching is truly *news* in the sense of re-imagining grace in their life here and now. It is *good* when it is consistent with the life-giving message of Jesus who proclaims the Realm of God in their midst.

In calling myself a preacher-witness, I draw on the four images used by Redemptorist James Wallace to delineate the role of the preacher: herald, witness, teacher, and interpreter.[5] The example of witness stands closest to my understanding of preaching. The witness is one who has experienced something outside of self and is willing to testify to it as foundational in his or her life precisely because what has been experienced touches something profound in the self. The witness does not prove anything, but becomes *proof* in the preaching moment in his or her manifestation of authenticity or character (André Resner's *ēthos*[6]). Theology cannot prove God's existence but only hope to alert us mystically to the intimations of God in our experience. God is always already here.

Thomas Long also uses the term *witness* to describe the role of the preacher. In his book, *The Witness of Preaching,* he writes: 'The witness is not a neutral observer. The truth is larger than the witness's own experience of it, and the witness is always testifying to a gospel larger than the preacher's personal faith, but the witness preacher *has* experienced it at some depth and is thereby involved in it.'[7]

This witness is an act of reminding or remembering. One of the tasks of the preacher is to look ahead while *reminding* the listeners of the presence of God in all of life's events, especially those of the past. The Catholic tradition, replete with ritual and sacrament, conveys well this memorial proclamation. Blessed with memory, the preacher joyfully anticipates the expanding horizon of the Realm of God. David Buttrick calls this 'true *anamnesis* [which] stands on tiptoe.'[8]

Buttrick calls preachers 'pulpit poets' whose task it is to image a new world: 'They shape the newness of God's *basileia* in faith consciousness. In so doing, they preach the preaching of Jesus Christ, for they declare the [Realm] of God.'[9] 'Good heavens,' he writes, '[preachers] actually open a doorway in!'[10]

---

[5] James Wallace, *Imaginal Preaching: An Archetypal Perspective* (New York: Paulist, 1995), 10–15.

[6] André Resner Jr, *Preacher and Cross: Person and Message in Theology and Rhetoric* (Grand Rapids, MI/Cambridge, UK: William B Eerdmans, 1999).

[7] Thomas Long, *The Witness of Preaching* (Louisville: Westminster John Knox, 1989), 56.

[8] David Buttrick, *Preaching the New and the Now* (Louisville: Westminster John Knox, 1998), 112.

[9] *Ibid.*, 100.

[10] *Ibid.*

I am consistent with the apostolic thrust of Redemptorists to the extent that I preach in order to help bring about continual conversion as well as renewed appreciation for the sacraments and participation in the life of the Church. If Alphonsus had made explicit a Christian anthropology, he would have had it mean nothing apart from Jesus, his cross, and prayer, 'the great means of salvation'. As Francis Schüssler Fiorenza notes, 'Our access to the person of Christ is mediated by his salvific deeds.'[11] As men on mission, Redemptorists are witnesses to the Proclaimer when we preach the in-breaking of the Realm of God, in season and out, here and now, in the concrete issues and situations of this life. We are balanced preachers when we 'bear witness to the revealing God in such a way as to sustain a meaningful dialogue with the contemporary experience of God's hiddenness, absence, eclipse, or death.'[12] If living the fullness of God's Realm is the mountain, then the suffering and obedience of the cross constitute the hiddenness of the summit. What is required is absolute faith in God's love and presence, despite our blindness in the midst of this 'unapproachable light'. Preachers help elucidate the path to God when both naming grace (Mary Catherine Hilkert) and naming evil (Philip Wogman).[13]

Excellent preaching taps into the poverty and prosperity of a people. The congregation will still hear the Spirit speaking after the preacher sits down if the words of the homily rest on 'the materiality of the listener's world', if the preacher has truly 'proclaimed the Spirit in the world the listeners know.'[14] Thomas Troeger wants preachers to help others 'climb up into the truths of their lives.'[15] It is a question of authenticity, whose value comes only from the freedom of life in Christ. For God's presence to be freely offered and accepted, it must be made and accepted in a free human subject.[16] Douglas John Hall reminds us, though, that irresponsible and selfish freedom is nothing more than tyranny.[17] For Christian preaching must attempt to effect a responsible freedom and a christological authenticity in and through the Spirit who (rather than the preacher) has the 'last word' by helping to

---

[11] Francis Schüssler Fiorenza and John P Galvin, eds., *Systematic Theology: Roman Catholic Perspectives,* vol. 1 (Minneapolis: Fortress, 1991), 315.

[12] Hall, 47.

[13] Philip J Wogman, *Speaking the Truth in Love: Prophetic Preaching to a Broken World* (Louisville: Westminster John Knox, 1998), 52-54.

[14] Thomas Troeger, *Creating Fresh Images for Preaching* (Valley Forge, PA: Judson, 1982), 39.

[15] *Ibid.*, 30.

[16] Fiorenza, 40.

[17] Douglas John Hall, *Professing the Faith: Christian Theology in a North American Context* (Minneapolis: Fortress, 1993), 25.

spell out in the lives of the listeners the Good News that the preacher witnesses with the voice.[18]

So, to whom is the preacher-witness responsible? Ultimately, we are responsible to God who first called us to this witness. We are also responsible to the community of believers, to whom we now figuratively turn.

The turn to community

To be is to be related. Yahweh's name, 'I am', is also 'I will be for you'. The divine covenant not only links us to God, but essentially to one another. The first great commandment is love of God; the second great commandment is love of neighbor. Karl Rahner writes, 'We cannot do anything else than see our own fate in the fate of our neighbour.'[19]

Our freedom, coming from the Spirit of the Proclaimer, is ordered toward the community. The question has graduated from 'freedom from what?' to 'freedom for what?' to 'freedom for whom?'. Sandra Schneiders argues that the Christian community is the 'place of encounter' between Jesus and his disciples, indeed the ongoing incarnational presence of Christ in the world today: 'The task of the community is to be, through love, Jesus' bodily presence, and thus the giver of his Spirit, to all who will come to believe down through the ages.'[20]

An operative theology of preaching for a Redemptorist never rests until proclamation stirs the hearts of the listeners and galvanizes a community for self-reflection and praxis. It is written that Alphonsus would stay in a parish long enough so that any feuds between families were resolved and a town's peace restored. The joy of a mission accomplished comes from leaving a community with a clear sense of who they are and where God is leading them in their common life in Christ. This type of ministry changes the preacher so that he may, in the words of the 1996 general chapter of the Redemptorists, 'evangelize the poor and *be evangelized by the poor*.' As a mission preacher, I understand this two-way evangelization when I tune my ear to the fears, obsessions, and toxic theologies of people who speak with me, even as I am most humbled and inspired by the depth of spirituality and keen sense of awareness of God in the lives of many.

---

[18] Troeger, 58.

[19] Karl Rahner, 'Jesus, Man, and the Church', trans. Margaret Kohl, *Theological Investigations*, vol. 17, (London: Darton, Longman and Todd, 1981), 32.

[20] Sandra Schneiders, *Written That You May Believe: Encountering Jesus in the Fourth Gospel* (New York: Crossroad, 1999), 62.

The author of the first letter of John knew this joy when he wrote:

> This is what we proclaim to you: what was from the beginning,
> what we have heard, what we have seen with our eyes, what
> we have looked upon and our hands have touched—we speak
> of the Word of life. (This life became visible; we have seen and
> bear witness to it, and we proclaim to you the eternal life that
> was present to the Father and became visible to us.) What we
> have seen and heard we proclaim in turn to you so that you
> may share life with us. This fellowship of ours is with the Father
> and with his Son, Jesus Christ. Indeed, our purpose in writing
> you this is that our joy may be complete.[21]

Preaching is not so much building up God's Realm (God alone
expands horizons), but rather creating the condition possible for 'stepping
into' the Realm of God through witnessing to the Proclaimer by loving
participation in the lives of others. In this way God's Realm is an experience
of a loving, saving, abiding God in this life and a promise of the continuation
of that life in the future. David Buttrick writes on this point:

> Preaching is more than a recital of 'holy history' from the past.
> Preaching participates in the shaping of consciousness and thus
> in the reconstruction of a social world. Our preaching is thus
> involved in God's redemptive work. ... When Jesus preached
> the [Realm of God], his presence was a kind of imminence
> pressing against his first-century world. We who continue his
> proclamation are also a voice of God's future addressing our
> contemporary world.[22]

I find great hope from the efficacy of words in the preaching
moment. Blessed and burdened by the responsibility to be a faithful witness
to Jesus and the Realm of God, as a preacher I take seriously the connection
between theology (what I say) and rhetoric (how I say it). My words, coming
from deep within myself, are God's words and expressions of God's creative
Spirit, the breath of life.

In the evolving lingo of historical consciousness, we have progressed
from a 'turn to the subject' to the 'socio-political turn' to the 'linguistic turn'.
The 'turn to the community' is the next necessary step. In the turn to the

---

[21] 1 John 1: 1-4 *NAB*.
[22] Buttrick, 82.

community we make incarnate God's Realm on this side of the grave, through the practice of harmonious relationship with others and with all of creation.

Ruined if we do not preach

Recently, the Superior General of the Redemptorists issued a statement entitled 'I Am Ruined If I Do Not Preach' (1 Cor. 9: 16).[23] It was Alphonsus' wish that the Congregation of the Most Holy Redeemer never take parishes or teach in schools—so dominant were missions in his vision. However, because of leadership needs in 1832 when the first confreres came upon North American shores and were asked to pastor parishes, Redemptorists have been at times understandably more concerned about 'the care of souls' than performing the first work of our institute—mission preaching for continual conversion. Looking back over the past one hundred and fifty years, I have come to realize that the evangelization we do on missions is of vital service to the Church in the United States. Our identity as a congregation would seriously be threatened were this ministry to be neglected. Just as the people who lowered their friend through the roof to be healed were without a doubt also 'touched' by Jesus, so Redemptorists, similarly influenced by the Redeemer, have much to proclaim in our unique witness of him in our lives. Our task is to accompany people up the mountain to get a better view of the Realm of God in their lives, so that when they find themselves in the valley of the shadow of pain, confusion, death, or some other darkness, they may recognize that God is there as well. This is heaven on earth, the in-breaking of the Realm, God's grace actualized so that all may have life abundantly.

The pulpit is a mountain. The preaching moment supplies the necessary experience of liminality, the 'between space' or threshold for the encounter with God. Isaiah captures this so well:

> On this mountain the Lord of hosts will make for all peoples a feast of rich food, a feast of well-aged wines, of rich food filled with marrow, of well-aged wines strained clear. And he will destroy on this mountain the shroud that is cast over all peoples, the sheet that is spread over all nations; he will swallow up death forever. Then the Lord God will wipe away the tears from all faces, and the disgrace of his people he will take away

---

[23] *Communicanda* #2 (Rome: 1999).

from all the earth, for the Lord has spoken. It will be said on that day, Lo, this is our God; we have waited for him, so that he might save us. This is the Lord for whom we have waited; let us be glad and rejoice in his salvation. For the hand of the Lord will rest on this mountain.[24]

---

[24] Isaiah 25: 6-9 *NRSV.*

COME AND SEE
Michael A Becker

My vision for a preaching ministry relates directly to my present position as Director of Vocations. It is a vision shaped by the serious attention that one must give to the situation of the hearer of the Word. The vocation preaching ministry will be effective only in the measure that preachers are increasingly aware of the anguish and struggle and thirsts of the human family and particularly the situation and thirsts of those who are seeking to understand the direction and purpose of their lives. Otherwise, what we preach may be an answer to a question no one is asking. The situation of the hearer is biblically described in the book of Psalms: 'O God, you are my God whom I seek; for you my flesh pines and my soul thirsts, like the earth, parched, lifeless and without water.'[1]

In reflecting upon the teachings of Mother Theresa of Calcutta, a priest of her community notes in an unpublished manuscript that the whole of revelation is summed up in the words of Jesus from the cross: 'I thirst.' Christ, representative of the human family (particularly the poorest of the poor), thirsts for a love that can only be found in God. The dry, weary land of our souls thirsts for the living God. 'I thirst', spoken by Jesus from between the thieves, captures metaphorically the deep longings of the human person, identifying the hearer as one in profound need of God's grace. I thirst for love, for meaning, for a sense of belonging. This is surely the thirst of the young in our contemporary culture, and this thirst must be addressed by the vocation ministers if they are to be effective proclaimers of Christ's call to service of the Church and the human family.

In Christ is revealed the depth of humanity's thirst for God. The preacher is the one who names the thirsts of those who gather for worship. In Christ is also revealed the living water of God, flowing down upon the dry weary land of our hearts. He is the living water given to the Samaritan woman

---

[1] Ps. 63: 2 *NAB*.

at the well. Christ himself proclaims on the last and greatest day of the festival, 'If anyone thirsts, let him come to me; let him drink who believes in me. Scripture has it: from within him rivers of living water shall flow.'[2] This sensitivity to the position of the hearer is of particular importance to the preacher of vocations, not because hearers are necessarily the poor and alienated, but that they too experience deep longings for purpose and direction.

Christ's 'I thirst', revealing humanity's thirst for the living God, reveals as well God's thirsting love for humanity. The preaching community is particularly sensitive to the thirsting love of God for the world, a love that is revealed in word and sacrament, which declare both sanctification and justification for the hearer. This community of preachers also invites those who thirst to grow in a faith that recognizes the love of God lying hidden in the struggle and the longing of their lives. The hearer is invited to name the thirst as grace, as a longing for God in the depth of the heart. Hearers who are searching for direction and meaning in life will appreciate the way that the preacher enables them to name that thirst, and they will in openness desire to satisfy it in the call of Christ to discipleship.

Preaching the gospel of vocation

It is increasingly evident to me that my present ministry as a diocesan director of vocations is one that has preaching as its foundation. I am now most often preaching 'vocations', whether in the context of a discernment retreat for young university students, a weekend of masses in a parish, or a school mass for vocations. I find the scriptural paradigm for vocation ministry in the call of Andrew and Peter. Upon hearing John the Baptist proclaim the Lamb of God, they follow Jesus, who turns and asks, 'What do you seek?' They reply, 'Rabbi, where are you staying?' Jesus responds, 'Come and see.'[3] In the words of John Paul II, 'The proper dynamism of this personal call develops in the phases of seeking Christ, finding him, and staying with him.'[4]

My ministry in vocations is to care for the birth, discernment, and fostering of vocations. It flows from my own sense of having been called to the priesthood. I recognize myself as one who seeks and finds and stays with Christ. Beyond my desire to witness to my personal call, however, this concern for vocations 'is a connatural and essential dimension of the Church's pastoral work. The reason for this is that vocation, in a certain sense, defines the very

---

[2] John 7: 37b-38 *NAB*.
[3] John 1: 35-39.
[4] John Paul II, *I Will Give You Shepherds* (Boston: Pauline Books and Media, 2000), 65.

being of the Church.'[5] As the Church of Christ, we are an assembly of those whom the Lord has called.

My ministry of vocational preaching challenges me to first reflect upon the call that is given to all members of the Church to seek and find and stay with Christ. More specifically, however, I am to companion the young in their search for Christ, a search that is rooted in the thirsts for meaning and purpose in life. It is a thirst for community. God's reign will come about as individuals are drawn together into a living community of faith and accept God's invitation to abide with him. The longing for the intimacy, the longing to 'stay with', is one of the deep thirsts of the human person. My call to preach is the call to build up the body of Christ, to invite the hearer to recognize his or her unique place within the human family, and to know that it is in this living Body that one's thirsts are ultimately satisfied. It is within that communion that a specific call to ministry can be heard.

My preaching of vocations is integrally connected to my role as presider at the Eucharist. My preaching is an invitation to this banquet of life. It is at this banquet that our hunger and thirst is satisfied, and it is from this banquet that we go forth to satisfy the hunger and thirst of others. As the prophet Isaiah proclaims, 'All you who are thirsty, come to the water! ... Come to me heedfully, listen, that you may have life.'[6]

The call to ministry is a call to servant leadership in this community. Christ's invitation to 'stay with me' is certainly the call to enter fully the communion of his mystical body. As a priest finds those needs met within the community of faith, he becomes, through his own preaching and pastoral ministry, an agent of this community for others. If Christ is not for me the living water, and if my thirst is not slaked in the community to which he calls me, I will speak unconvincingly and ineffectively.

To be effective in the proclamation of the gospel message of vocations, it is essential to understand the contemporary climate of our culture and church. It is within this climate or milieu that the hearer is either receptive to a theology of call or deaf to its challenge. In the first chapter of the apostolic exhortation, *I Will Give You Shepherds*, published at the conclusion of a synod on priestly formation, Pope John Paul offers an exceptionally insightful reflection on the 'challenges facing priestly formation at the conclusion of the second millennium'. While his thoughts reflect his concerns for the Church universal, his analyses of the contemporary milieu are particularly apropos for North America. He asks very pointedly, 'What are the positive and negative elements in socio-cultural and ecclesial contexts that affect boys, adolescents, and young men who throughout their lives are called to bring to maturity a

---

[5] *Ibid.*

[6] Isa. 55: 1, 3 *NAB*.

project of priestly life?'[7] The answer to this question is critical. John Paul spells out in his answer the opportunities and threats, strengths and weaknesses with which the vocation preacher must deal.

Ever a man of hope, Pope John Paul begins by naming the positive elements which define our social and ecclesial culture:

> A number of factors seem to be working toward making people today more deeply aware of the dignity of the human person and more open to religious values, to the gospel, and to priestly ministry. ... Society is increasingly witnessing a powerful thirst for justice and peace; a more lively sense that humanity must care for creation and respect nature; a more open search for truth; a greater effort to safeguard human dignity. ... There is a new call for ethics, that is, a quest for meaning—and therefore for an objective standard of values which will delineate the possibilities and limits of progress. There is evident an increasing love for the Sacred Scriptures, ... and a thirst for God and for an active meaningful relationship with him.[8]

Ever the realist, John Paul notes, as well, the many problematic and negative elements at work in our secular culture: there is a rationalism that

> renders human reason insensitive to an encounter with revelation and with divine transcendence ..., a desperate defense of personal subjectivity which tends to close it off in individualism, rendering it incapable of true human relationships. ... And there is spreading in every part of the world a sort of practical and existential atheism which coincides with a secularist outlook on life and human destiny.[9]

In our ecclesial culture, he observes a

> lack of due knowledge of the faith in many believers, a catechesis with little practical effect, ... a persistent diffidence and almost unacceptance of the magisterium ... and the tendencies to reduce the richness of the Gospel message ... into an element of exclusively human and social liberation.[10]

---

[7] John Paul II, 14.
[8] *Ibid.*
[9] *Ibid.*, 15, 16.
[10] *Ibid.*, 17.

It is to this audience, in this milieu of both light and darkness, that the gospel of vocation is proclaimed. It is within this context that one must frame a theology of vocations that builds upon the promise held out in our culture and addresses the darker dimensions that need to be dispelled by the light of the Gospel. The preaching of the gospel of vocation must be carried out in a way which honors the goodness which is present in the hearer, which honors the sacred and yet unnamed desires which animate and give life to the hearer. It is the model of sacramental imagination that allows us to name the grace of vocation present in another.

Naming the primacy of grace in vocation

What is the Church doing when it preaches? And more to the point in my own ministry of preaching vocations, what am I about when I proclaim as gospel the call to public service and whole-hearted discipleship, rooted in personal communion with Jesus Christ?

A genuine theology of preaching must take into account the method in which God's Word is proclaimed, as well as a careful consideration of the preacher. I shall address each with appropriate light shed upon the mission of proclaiming vocation.

Mary Catherine Hilkert, in *Naming Grace: Preaching and the Sacramental Imagination*, gives a sound historical perspective on preaching, contrasting the dialectical imagination of the Reformed tradition and the sacramental imagination of the Catholic tradition. Led by such great preachers as Karl Barth and Rudolf Bultmann, the dialectical approach has as its great strength its focus upon the power and efficacy of the Word of God, itself a cause of grace. The role of the preacher is to announce to the world what God has done in the person of Christ. Preaching in this tradition brings the hearer into a direct encounter with Christ. Confronted by the challenge of the Gospel, the hearer is led to the point of decision. In my present vocation ministry, it is evident that preaching offers a personal invitation to servant leadership, and confronts the hearer with the challenge to action. 'Come follow me'—the words of Jesus himself—are words that command obedience and decision.

The preaching theology of Dietrich Bonhoeffer forcibly acknowledges the presence of Christ in the proclamation itself, noting that 'the whole Christ is present in preaching, Christ humiliated and Christ exalted.'[11] The living Christ, then, issues the call to discipleship in preaching.

---

[11] Dietrich Bonhoeffer, *Worldly Preaching: Lectures on Homiletics* (New York: Crossroads, 1991), 21.

An operative preaching theology for the vocation director must have a dialectical nuance, for it is Christ himself who issues the call to discipleship, a word that the discerning Christian longs to hear. It is that word of grace to which a young person humbly yet courageously responds.

Mary Catherine Hilkert speaks of preaching as the 'art of naming grace found in the depth of human experience'.[12] This approach to preaching is grounded in an abiding faith that grace is present in all of creation. This theology of grace, reflective of the sacramental imagination, is most fully developed by the Catholic theologian Karl Rahner, of whom Herbert Vorgrimler writes:

> From his own experience there arose a basic theological conviction that God has revealed himself to every human being and that this is the authentic and most original form of revelation. Therefore it does not need special bearers of the mystery who control it; rather, sometimes it needs a kind of midwife, since not all human beings are in a position to understand and interpret their lives, and what happens to them.[13]

The role of the preacher, in proclaiming a gospel of vocation, is thus to enable the hearers to interpret the fundamentally graced nature of their lives and in this to discern the calling that they have received as children of God. Young persons discerning the voice of Christ to service in the Church are invited by this manner of preaching to pay greater attention to the moments of grace that draw them toward pastoral charity and toward recognition of the presence of the living God in the faces of the poor. They are invited in this approach to recognize the voice of Christ in the stirrings of their heart and in the words of invitation and encouragement which others are offering to them.

Contributing to a collection of essays entitled *Signatures of Grace*, the Catholic writer Murray Bodo tells of his own calling to holy orders, recognizing that it was in the sacredness of the ordinary that he heard the call of Christ: 'All of creation is an immense sacrament. All created things are signs of God that we decipher in order to find our way to God. The medieval Franciscan Saint Bonaventure put it this way: "Every creature is a word of God."'[14] In growing appreciation of the sacramental nature of reality, he notes the change

---

[12] Mary Catherine Hilkert, *Naming Grace: Preaching and the Sacramental Imagination* (New York: Continuum, 1997), 44.

[13] Herbert Vorgrimler, *Understanding Karl Rahner: An Introduction to His Life and Thought* (New York: Crossroad, 1986), 23.

[14] Murray Bodo, in *Signatures of Grace: Catholic Writers on the Sacraments*, ed. Thomas Grady and Paula Huston (New York: Penguin Putnam, 2000), 189.

that occurs in those who are graced with this imagination: 'We begin with the sacraments, we live them, we begin to see sacramental signs everywhere, we end up becoming ourselves "sacraments" of God's presence.'[15]

The preacher of vocations, then, is one who is able to find the words to open up the greater sacred realities present in the life of the hearer, naming absolute primacy of grace in vocation: 'You did not choose me but I chose you. And I appointed you to go and bear fruit, fruit that will last.'[16]

At this point, it is valuable to consider how the character of the preacher affects the preaching ministry. In his particularly insightful book, *Preacher and Cross*, André Resner Jr offers an historical and rhetorical analysis of the notion of *ēthos*, having to do with the real and perceived moral character of the speaker.[17] The person of the preacher, particularly a priest who is preaching a gospel of vocation, is actually inviting hearers to 'imitate me.' Here the character of the preacher is at the heart of the proclamation itself. Resner considers the manner in which the apostle Paul invited his hearers to observe that he was himself living the life of the crucified one. Resner looks at Paul's embrace of the cross as the key to his credibility in preaching. Paul's life of suffering, rather than being a stumbling block, was itself an embodiment of the message of Christ crucified.

The priest who is called to preach vocation must be particularly sensitive to aligning his person with his message. Karl Rahner as preacher and priest, using his sacramental imagination in a way that is self-revelatory, ponders the manner in which God is revealed to him and to others in his own humanity. He names grace as he humbly seeks to live the call of Christ both in word and action:

> But, O God of my calling, it would be easier if I could just deliver your message and then, when Your work is done, go back to living my own life. Then the burden of being your messenger would be no heavier than that of any other messenger or administrator who does his job and is done with it. But your charge to me, Your commission itself has become my very life. It ruthlessly claims all my energies for itself; it lives from my own life.[18]

The character of the preacher is poignantly described here. The

---

[15] *Ibid.*, 191.

[16] John 15: 16a *NRSV.*

[17] André Resner Jr, *Preacher and Cross: Person and Message in Theology and Rhetoric* (Grand Rapids, MI/Cambridge, UK: William B. Eerdmans, 1999).

[18] Karl Rahner. *Encounters With Silence*, trans. James M Demske (Westminster, MD: Newman, 1960), 72.

gospel message, in an incarnational fashion, actually draws its life from that of the preacher. Rahner continues:

> As your messenger, I can live my own personal life only by passing on Your word. I am your messenger and nothing more. Your lamp—excuse me for being so bold—burns with the oil of my life. ... And Your light continues to shine forth, changing the dark death-shadows of our earth into the brilliant noonday of your grace, even when this light has to find its way to men through the cracked and dusty pains of my tiny lantern.[19]

It is evident from Rahner's reflections that our rhetoric of self-revelation plays a crucial role in preaching. I am doing so much more in preaching than trying to persuade by my eloquence. As I invite the hearer to name the grace present in the ordinariness of life, a grace which calls us to extraordinary self-sacrifice, I am aware that my own ordinariness as a preacher is also the space where God's presence is to be acknowledged.

In awe at the 'Word made flesh' character of preaching, Rahner prays: 'How can I bring my hearers to distinguish between You and me in the frightful mixture of me that I call my sermons? How can I teach them to take Your word to their hearts, and forget me, the preacher?'[20] The answer is obvious: God's word and my life are inseparable. In his essay, 'Priest as Poet', Rahner writes:

> But daily life also forms a part of man, in which he effaces himself in all humility. The weariness of the small hours, in which man is banished from himself without being fully aware of his pitiable forlornness, is part of him. Therefore the word which he speaks in this his situation also forms a part of man as needing and meriting redemption. And for that reason the word of God has assumed this human word also. For all its truth and dignity, it can enter into the kenosis of the human word, into all its baseness and banality. The word of God too can take on the form of a slave.[21]

The preacher is one who most humbly acknowledges the need, in ordinary life, of redemption. Feeling called to assist others in interpreting

---

[19] *Ibid.*, 72-73.
[20] *Ibid.*, 74.
[21] Karl Rahner. *Theological Investigations: Volume III* (Baltimore: Helicon, 1967), 314.

their lives in the light of the Gospel, the preacher stands always as one who admits personally the need for faith, in a life at times dimly lit. In the vocation sermon, the rhetoric of the preacher's life reveals that this marvelous ministry is possessed only through God's mercy. With Paul, the vocation preacher believes, 'This treasure we possess in earthen vessels, to make it clear that its surpassing power comes from God and not from us.'[22]

Theological underpinnings

If the preacher of a theology of vocation is to be effective in addressing hearers at the dawn of this new millennium, that preacher must be aware of the seismic shifts that have been occurring in the way we look at God and Christ and one another. The preacher must be grounded in a theology that speaks of a God who remains faithful after a century of devastating suffering and chaos. The preacher must be grounded in a Christology that speaks of a God approachable as one of us in an age of pluralism. The preacher must be grounded in an anthropology that speaks to the sacred place of the human person in a cosmic village.

I would like to draw upon the significant work of the Catholic theologian Roger Haight—*Jesus, Symbol of God*—in describing the characteristics of the postmodern age. Haight writes, firstly: 'Postmodernity involves a radical historical consciousness. Gone is the confidence in progress, goals toward which history is heading, a *telos* that provides a destiny and gives a meaning to movement.'[23] We have edged toward the destruction of our planet. Our laws and cultures are not based upon any universally valid knowledge. There is little that it seems we can say about humankind and our direction and purpose.

Secondly, 'Postmodernity involves a critical social consciousness. Social scientists find that society is driven by little more than the interests of power, or class, or gender, or greed. This side of postmodernity threatens a loss of the human subject, of the person, who is reduced to a function of impersonal forces.'[24] Haight observes, however, that the dramatic negative experiences of the past century can likely mediate encounters with greater, transcendent values. Does not a more socially conscious world call for a new understanding of Christ and his mission?

Thirdly, 'Postmodernity involves a pluralistic consciousness. At no other time have people had such a sense of the difference of others, of the

---

[22] 2 Cor. 4: 7 *NAB*.

[23] Roger Haight, *Jesus, Symbol of God* (New York: Orbis, 1999), 331.

[24] *Ibid.*, 332.

pluralism of societies, cultures and religions, and of the relativity that this entails.'[25] In such a world, all is reduced to opinion, and young people find themselves unable to identify any universal or absolute principles. There are now no overarching stories that encompass all of humankind. Can we begin now to articulate a new relationship between Christians and the family of cultures?

Fourthly, 'Postmodernity involves a cosmic consciousness. Naïve anthropocentrism is dead. The new concern for our own planet has helped in this internalization of this cosmic consciousness.'[26] We no longer can place ourselves at the center of our universe. While our place within the cosmos is now relative, does this reorientation not actually give us a new perspective on our common humanity and our creatureliness?

Douglas John Hall, a Reformed theologian from Canada, while not articulating the challenges of postmodernity in quite the way that Haight does, nonetheless constructs an ecumenically sensitive theology which begins to address them. I would like to look now at a developing theology, Christology, and anthropology which acknowledges its historical roots, answers in an ecumenical fashion the questions posed by postmodernity, and relates each to the mission of the Church and to a developing theology of vocation, which has been our point of departure.

Our age cries out for a God who is near to us. The 'Father Almighty' image of God has left us wondering whether God is too much like our darker selves, seeking to dominate and to keep a safe distance from intimacy. In worshiping a God of power and might, we have made power and might the measure of our own godliness. This has too often revealed our ugliness. It is this image of God which has led to our need to dominate the planet and which has at times been used as justification for the past century of bloodshed. This has caused us to lose our sense of purpose and destiny, for our wars and dominance have only led to confusion and division. But without such an image of God, what can satisfy us? What longing remains? Hall rightly responds 'that God's being comprises an orientation toward "the other"—is God's being-*with*.'[27] The theology of glory, the basis for a triumphant Christendom, is replaced by an 'Emmanuel' theology, as we look to God as one who is in total solidarity with us. An 'ontology of communion' gives humanity its purpose—namely, to live in communion with a 'suffering God'. The person becomes subject again, as one freed by a God who is one with us and within

---

[25] *Ibid.*, 333.

[26] *Ibid.*, 334.

[27] Douglas John Hall, *Professing the Faith: Christian Theology in a North American Context* (Minneapolis: Fortress, 1993), 147.

us. Our growing cosmic consciousness invites us to see this God-with-us as being with all of creation, as well.

As a constitutive element of a theology of vocation, a renewed understanding of God-with-us can resonate more deeply with young people in our culture who have a growing sense of solidarity with the marginalized and who have come to thrive in a multicultural and religiously pluralistic society. The young man called to the priesthood will recognize his own identification, not with the Father almighty, but with the Father of the orphan and the poor.

A theology of vocation is fundamentally christocentric. The preacher of vocations must assist the hearer in answering the question 'Who do you say that I am?' Even more pertinently, the preacher must lead the hearer to ask Dietrich Bonhoeffer's question, 'Who is Jesus Christ for me today?'

If we move from the Father Almighty to a God-with-us, then our age demands that we move from an image of Christ the King to Christ-for-us. As Haight notes, 'The term "salvation" refers to the most fundamental of all Christian experiences ..., though the Church has never formulated a conciliar definition of salvation nor provided a universally accepted conception.'[28] Haight goes on to ask, 'Given the plurality of conceptions, is there a way systematically to establish a center of gravity on the salvation mediated by Jesus that will be clear and definite but open and not exclusive?'[29] In answering this question, Douglas John Hall correctly observes: 'It is possible to show an almost exact correlation between the human predicament, as it was perceived in the varying historical situations concerned, and the manner in which the Church articulated the meaning of the atonement.'[30] In his historical analysis of the various theories of atonement or salvation, Hall clearly suggests a methodology for answering the christological question. One first considers the human predicament of postmodernism, as sketched above by Haight, and then one seeks a correlative understanding of the place of Christ in a postmodern world. For Hall, we are to move beyond the classical theories of atonement, for they do not speak clearly to our postmodern mentality. Rather, in our world burdened by the anxiety of meaningless, a new *imago Christi* is to be proclaimed. Drawing upon the metaphor of 'representation', Hall suggests: 'Jesus accepts as his destiny the representation of a creature deeply estranged from its Creator, profoundly disoriented in all its relationships, and, apart from radical grace, destroying itself from within.'[31] The truest name for Jesus is Emmanuel, God-with-us in the face of a world mired in pessimism

---

[28] Haight, 335.

[29] *Ibid.*, 336.

[30] Hall, 403.

[31] *Ibid.*, 544.

and purposelessness, issuing the imperative for socially responsible behavior in a pluralistic society.

We are emerging from a modern age which so strongly emphasized the independence and accomplishments of the human family. The ego of modernity has fed upon our mastery of this world, and our achievements have been enshrined as a testimony that we can live as if God does not exist or as if our achievements are a divine reward for our greatness. The question with which we are faced, however, is this: What is the truly human? Is the glorious, deified image of the human, so long maintained by Christendom and enshrined by modernity, serviceable to a postmodern era? Neither Haight nor Hall think so. The twentieth century has had a sobering effect upon the attentive. In the culture of the United States of America, we can perhaps point to the Vietnam War as the beginning of a serious reassessment. We do not suffer defeat well. As Hall observes, 'What our Christian anthropology has not been able to do for us is to incorporate the experience of radical failure into itself in such a way that we might find in it a framework of meaning for our actual failures.'[32] In its most abbreviated form, 'The failure in question is a failure to perceive human life as being purposeful.'[33] This is true for today's youth, for whom purpose and direction have been sacrificed on the Nietzschean 'abyss of indeterminacy'.[34] The challenge is great for anyone seeking to inspire young people to a sense of noble purpose and sacred calling.

What is it to be human? The Promethean rhetoric which has placed humanity above ordinary nature must give way to a language that honors humankind's place within the whole of creaturely being. The language of domination must give way to a language of dominion, not as exemplified by Caesar, but rather as by Christ.[35] The human vocation is truly the vocation of Christ, to 'represent to all creatures the God who "is love," … and as well to represent all creatures before God.'[36] Here is given an image of discipleship which may surely resonate with those who are disenchanted with the failed image of domination. It is a representational vocation 'understood as sacrificial servanthood, … expressed chiefly in the language of gratitude, thanksgiving, and praise.'[37] Indeed, this image of the human person invites the future priest to see his place as one among equals in the human family. 'Far from removing

---

[32] *Ibid.*, 284.

[33] *Ibid.*, 285.

[34] Haight, 332.

[35] Hall, 351.

[36] *Ibid.*, 352.

[37] *Ibid.*

the human creature from the rest of creation, the stewardly, priestly, and poetic vocation of humankind as it is understood within this tradition presses toward an even greater sense of being-with in relation to the others.'[38] The preacher of vocations can draw upon this noble image of the human person as a model for an authentic priestly life.

---

[38] *Ibid.*, 353.

CREATE A RIGHT RELATIONSHIP
David G Morman

My first recollections about God were images of God as the Father Almighty and the God of power, a God defined as the supreme ruler and judge. God was the creator and master of all that had been created. These images have some basis in our Christian tradition, and they were reinforced by my being raised as a child of a career soldier in the United States Army, which has an emphasis on power, duty, and obedience. This all-mighty and all-powerful God was somehow linked to the United States of America: the nation that was based on liberty and justice for all, the nation that kept order and peace in the world, the nation that fought the evil regimes of communism and socialism. These images of God were echoed in patriotic anthems and slogans—'one nation under God', 'in God we trust', 'the land of the free', 'the land of opportunity', and 'God bless America'. Douglas John Hall names this God the 'God of glory'.[1]

North Dakota

This 'God of glory' came with me to Glen Ullin—a small, rural town in southwestern North Dakota where my parents were born and raised—after my father retired from the military and engaged in farming and ranching. Life on the farm and in the fields presented a different type of God—God, the creator, the one who gave creation its beauty and power. The power of this God was associated with bringing life into the world when crops were planted and grew and when calves were born in the spring and matured. The seed was planted, sprouted, grew, and brought forth an abundant harvest—grain that would be a source of income and used to feed people or animals. The

---

[1] Douglas John Hall, *Professing the Faith: Christian Theology in a North American Context* (Minneapolis: Fortress, 1993), 108-25.

calves grew, were weaned, sent to the feedlot, and eventually became another source of income and food for the human community. I was surrounded by the power of nature and its cycle of life and death and could only marvel at the intrinsic beauty of the process and the beauty of the rolling plains.

In this rural setting, I was introduced to the concept of stewardship— all belonged to God, we had to care for the cropland and pasture so that next year, and in the years to come, the earth would once again give life. Stewardship also meant we could not control nature or God. There were years of drought and no crop; there were harsh winters that killed livestock and wildlife. As a farmer and rancher, one could only hope that next year one would have a crop and livestock to sell.

In America, with its emphasis on 'property rights', stewardship becomes a challenge. A stewardship ethic views property differently: land is valued for its own sake. It becomes more proper to speak of 'working with' the land rather than 'using' the land. To preserve the integrity of creation as a gift from God, human beings are called to be responsible stewards—the web of life includes all that has been created.

Environmental issues in North Dakota have attracted much attention in the past year. The federal government has proposed changes in the way the National Grasslands are managed, and debate regarding lignite coal-fired plants to produce electricity continues to surface. In western North Dakota there are 1.2 million acres of National Grasslands, land owned by the government and leased to ranchers for summer pasture. The proposed changes would limit access to these lands and would take away land that had been used for summer pasture. For some ranchers it would mean the end of their ranching. The debate with the coal plants centers on the burning of lignite coal, a coal that burns inefficiently and causes more pollution than other types of coal. Discussions regarding the feasibility of wind-generated electricity have made headlines in regional newspapers. These are some of the environmental issues that western North Dakotans must face in the coming years; these are issues of stewardship that need to be addressed by the Church as it witnesses to the integrity of all creation.

Growing up, I heard different titles given to Jesus: Son of God, Messiah, Lord, Savior, and Son of Man. These titles were hard for me to understand. Yet, through work on the farm and in the fields, I came to know Jesus as my companion and friend. There were days when I worked alone in the fields, not seeing anyone for hours at a time. While doing fieldwork, I would converse with Jesus, talking to him about my life and telling him whatever was on my mind. I did this for eight years while doing the fieldwork of spring, summer, and fall. This work ended when I graduated from high school and enrolled in college.

It must be noted that in the years since I lived on the farm times have changed. The advent of technology and a revolution in agricultural methods have given a different face to rural North Dakota and much of rural America. Many small, family farms have ceased to exist, and operating farms are beset by financial woes. Towns once filled with people have become ghost towns. The countryside is being depopulated as people, especially young college graduates, move to larger cities such as Bismarck, Fargo, Minneapolis, Denver, Phoenix, and Las Vegas to secure employment. The remaining small towns struggle to maintain their schools, stores, and churches.[2] As a pastor in the country, I, along with others, begin to ask, 'Where is God in all of this?'

The summer of 1981 was a time of crisis for me. In the three months following my graduation from high school both my paternal grandparents died—my first encounter with the death of loved ones. I was raised in a pious Catholic family, which instilled into me the following characteristics: follow the ten commandments; help your neighbor; be kind, polite, and generous; obey parents and elders; and have a love for the clergy and religious and a devotion to the Church. 'I had done all these things from my youth,'[3] and I still suffered and grieved the death of my grandparents. God was somehow with me, but I did not know how.

After much soul-searching, counsel from my academic advisor, and solace from the chaplain at school, I said to myself, 'I want my life to make a difference in the world.' This statement would be the beginning of new way of looking at God, Jesus, creation, and life in general; it was the beginning of my call to holy orders in the Roman Catholic Church.

Discipleship

In college, I read *The Cost of Discipleship* by Dietrich Bonhoeffer, a book that forced me to ask questions regarding the discipleship called for by Jesus in the Gospels. 'What does it mean to take a courageous stance in the world because of my relationship to Jesus' became the question for me to search and ponder. Other events also gave different insights into discipleship. I encountered missionaries from Africa and Latin America who spoke of their experiences in 'the mission'; I learned of people like Martin Luther King Jr, who called for equality and justice in America because we are all children of God; I heard reports of people like Archbishop Oscar Romero, who were

---

[2] For further explanation, see Ken C Brovald, *Silent Towns on the Prairie: North Dakota's Disappearing Towns and Farms* (Missoula, MT: Pictorial Histories, 1999).

[3] Mark 10: 10 *NJB*.

assassinated for standing on the side of the poor. These events made me aware that discipleship, living out the values of the Reign of God embodied in Jesus, could have a price: one's life.

I was learning that there is more to Jesus than being his friend. I could not close my eyes to the world and have a comfortable Jesus-and-me relationship. Jesus grew from being my companion and friend to being the gift of God to the world.

> The world, for whose future this one sacrificed his own, is the context whose ongoing life is always in some measure—for faith—the scene of the life of the risen Christ. The resurrection … is a reality to be experienced in the living of life within this world. It means entering into worldly life … for faith expects to meet the redeemer there. Without waxing romantic about worldly wonders and delights; without closing its eyes to all that is ugly, evil, and dangerous; without expecting miraculous occurrences and signs and signs and wonders, faith enters the world with hope, believing that despite, in, and through all the bleak and negating as well as good and delightful things it finds there, there is a presence that is transforming death into life.[4]

In Jesus, God expresses solidarity with us even to the point of death. Walter Kasper writes, 'On the cross the incarnation of God reaches its truest meaning and purpose. God's self-emptying, his weakness and his sufferings … [are] an expression of his freedom; suffering does not befall God, rather he freely allows it to touch him.'[5]

The one who is fully human, Jesus, represents God to the created world, and he represents the fallen world to the God who redeems. As Elizabeth Johnson puts it, 'In our time, with our awareness of the compassionate nature of his ministry, and with our reading of the cross as the event where God's solidarity with those who suffer came to an unsurpassed focus, we can say of Jesus that the divine quality of the Compassion of God became incarnate in him.'[6]

---

[4] Hall, 493.

[5] Walter Kasper, *The God of Jesus Christ,* trans. Matthew J O'Connell (New York: Crossroad, 1986), 194-95.

[6] Elizabeth A Johnson, *Consider Jesus: Waves of Renewal in Christology* (New York: Crossroad, 1990), 126.

Jesus was raised from the dead by the power of God, who is life and love self-revealed, and the Holy Spirit was poured forth 'to renew human hearts and even the face of the earth'.[7] Jesus shows us the reality of a renewed life, the life that is the hope of all creation. Through the Holy Spirit, the Church is called to witness to the life of Jesus in its own time and circumstances.

The vision I have for myself as a preacher is to 'tell the truth'[8] about the way of Jesus and about life on the prairie, a life that has 'the tensions and the contradictions between hospitality and insularity, change and inertia, stability and instability, possibility and limitation, between open hearts and closed minds'.[9] The insularity, the inertia, the limitations, and the closed minds of people often find their roots in a lack of trust. It is feared that in facing the evil, ugly, and dangerous—really the darkness of life—that we will be overwhelmed and devoured by meaninglessness and negativity. The message of Jesus calls us to face this darkness with faith. Faith will reveal that we will not be destroyed but that we will learn the way of Jesus: in weakness power reaches perfection.

Right relationship

My mission as a preacher finds its home in rural North Dakota, a place Kathleen Norris calls 'the Cappadocia of North America, ... a place the rest of the world considers a barren waste.'[10] The county in which I live, Golden Valley County, comprises nearly eleven hundred square miles and a population of just over two thousand people—half of them Catholic. I am the only priest in the county; the nearest priest to me being forty-five miles away. I am called to live in solidarity with farmers and ranchers, small business owners and mechanics, teachers and child-care workers, public employees of the county and state, and a substantial number of retired, elderly women and men—just to name a few of the pilgrims with whom I journey through life. My mission challenges me to address the issues faced in daily life: birth, marriage, sickness, and death; rapid changes in agriculture and low prices for commodities such as wheat, barley, canola, and sunflower seeds; the issue of affordable health care (physical and mental) and access to it; and the issue of the out-migration of youth and those left behind, generally the elderly.

---

[7] Johnson, 141.

[8] From a quotation by Cardinal Suhard in Donald B Cozzens, *The Changing Face of the Priesthood* (Collegeville, MN: Liturgical, 2000), 15.

[9] Kathleen Norris, *Dakota: A Spiritual Geography* (New York: Houghton Mifflin, 1993), 7.

[10] *Ibid.*, 3.

As a preacher, I call people into 'right relationship'.[11] Right relationship is a broad term that begins with the premise that all creation is interrelated—the web of life coming from the divine creator who in turn calls for justice on the face of the earth. We are called to fidelity, to be in right relationship with God, with one another, with all creation.

Hall, who refers to right relationship as the 'ontology of communion',[12] writes:

> God, even God, in this tradition is not 'all alone', an entity, a being 'greater than whom none can be conceived,' and so on; God is rather the center and source of all relatedness, the ground of our human capacity for being-with, the counterpart from whose presence creatures can never really escape. And the creatures, all of them, from the smallest and invisible to the planets and interstellar spaces, are living things whose life is dependent upon their interaction. They combine, in ways that defy the human imagination, the principles of identity and distinction; so that their distinctive identity is sustained only so long as it is held in creative tension with their dependence upon the others. Perhaps, as James Lovelock has proposed, the planet itself is a living reality whose being is throughout relational.[13]

The concepts of right relationship and ontology of communion are not unique to Christianity. Native American spirituality also speaks of right relationship: 'We must create a "Right Relationship" between ourselves and God, and a "Right Relationship" between ourselves and others, and a "Right Relationship" between ourselves and nature.'[14] This spirituality believes that tension, anxiety, and lack of purpose or meaning result from a lack of right relationship.

Right relationship involves coming to an understanding of what it means to be human and, ultimately, what it means to be in relationship to

---

[11] The term comes from Lawrence Boadt in his presentation entitled 'The Biblical Foundations of Prophetic Justice' at a *Preaching the Just Word Workshop* sponsored by the Diocese of Bismarck in Medora, North Dakota, 3-8 September 2000.

[12] Hall, 317.

[13] Hall, 322, citing J E Lovelock, *Gaia: A New Look at Life on Earth* (New York/Oxford: Oxford UP, 1987).

[14] Reaves Nahwooks, 'A Native American Perspective', in *The Ongoing Journey Awakening Spiritual Life in At-Risk Youth,* Robert Coles, *et al.* (Boys Town, NE: Boys Town Press, 1995), 150.

God, others, and all of creation. I remember the first day of my first college philosophy class when the professor stated, 'Man (*sic*) is a rational animal, distinct from the rest of creation because of freedom and knowledge.' This description succinctly summarized my view of creaturely being up to that time in my life. In the same way that my understanding of God and Jesus has evolved, so has my understanding of creaturely being. The main issues have been to define 'freedom' and 'knowledge' and to reflect seriously on the reality of sin.

Initially, freedom meant the ability to do anything one pleases. One could choose good or evil, and, as a Christian, I had the obligation to choose the good, as I understood it at that time. Sin, then, was making a choice against the good.

Freedom and knowledge, the once defining factors of creaturely being, took on new meaning as I learned more about God and Jesus and as I had more life experience. I heard people speak of concepts like 'social sin' and 'systemic evil'. I read books by Dietrich Bonhoeffer, H Richard Niebuhr, Charles Curran, and Bernard Häring; I saw the sexual scandals that rocked the Church in St Paul and Minneapolis and throughout the United States; and I experienced through travel the wretched living conditions of so many people in the world.

There was something wrong with our nation, a nation often defined by materialism and consumerism, and our world, a world in which so many people were stripped of their human dignity by the choices of others. Freedom and knowledge had to mean something else, and sin had to be acknowledged as a reality that demanded a response.

Hall's description of freedom has contributed in my evolving understanding of freedom: freedom is humanity in relationship with 'otherkind'.[15] The other may be God, humanity, or all of creation. Bonhoeffer states, 'In truth, freedom is a relationship between persons. Being free means "being free for the other."'[16] Freedom becomes associated with right relationship. As creaturely beings, we are not predestined or fated. Rather, we are invited into a relationship with the source of life itself, and that source of life will be faithful, even through death.

Knowledge becomes the ability to recognize right relationship as the basis of being human. As humans, we are mortal, finite, capable of sin, talented, gifted, and 'called to represent God before all creation'.[17] In other

---

[15] Hall, 330 *ff.*

[16] Dietrich Bonheoffer, *Creation and Fall: A Theological Interpretation of Genesis 1-3,* (New York, Macmillan, 1965), 37.

[17] Hall, 352.

words, we are called to a life of stewardship, tending to all that God has entrusted to us.

Using the gifts of freedom and knowledge in a responsible manner highlights a prime value for me: the importance of a well-formed conscience for the living of one's vocation as a creature and as a Christian. Conscience 'bears witness to the authority of truth in reference to the supreme Good to which the human person is drawn.'[18] Rules, laws, and regulations are important for the functioning of society and the Church, but they cannot take the place of a well-formed conscience that directs the creature to identify more closely with God who is freely and willingly, and without loss, self-revealing. So, too, in the giving of self to 'the other' in right relationship, one's identity will not be lost or negated.

Finally, sin must be acknowledged, and the call for conversion and transformation be made. The book of Hebrews stresses the total seriousness of conversion. We cannot command it at will. What is at issue is not daily repentance but the decisive change that is a 'new creation'.[19] God who creates desires the fullness life for creation, and God continually redeems so that the fullness of life may happen. As a preacher, I am one who is to call for conversion. I am to call people to see life as it is lived, to examine life in light of the Scriptures and the tradition of the Church so that right relationship may be established by the grace of God. This call to change and transformation is the call made by the prophets of old and Jesus himself. My prophetic voice as a preacher needs to echo the same call.

In addition to my current assignment as pastor of two rural parishes in Beach and in Golva, North Dakota, I also serve as chaplain at Home on the Range, a residential child-care facility owned and operated by the Diocese of Bismarck. This facility is designed to serve disadvantaged, neglected, problematic, abused, and delinquent adolescents, as well as those with chemical addictions. Home on the Range seeks to change the direction of the lives of its residents. This is done through a program called 'social skills', a program that teaches and reinforces the ability to be in right relationship. My call as chaplain, with other members of the staff, is to be credible, one whom the residents may trust. Robert Coles, a leading authority on the moral development of children, states that when trust is established, children at risk learn to make choices (to

---

[18] *Catechism of the Catholic Church,* #1777.

[19] Geoffrey W Bromiley, in *Theological Dictionary of the New Testament,* eds. Gerhard Kittel and Gerhard Friedrich, trans. and abridged in one vol. Geoffrey W Bromiley (Grand Rapids, MI: William B Eerdmans, reprinted 1992), 643.

use knowledge appropriately), and they learn how to figure out what matters (to use freedom).[20]

The issue of trust for me speaks of a life of integrity or, as André Resner would state, *ēthos* or character. The character of the preacher needs to be grounded in the Christian message, the scandal of the cross. In facing all that would negate life, we will not be overcome. We face the negation of life with faith, as Jesus did.[21] The scandal of the cross will rightly judge all that would negate life as evil. The way of the cross reveals our reliance on the providence of God, the call for loving concern for all, and attentiveness to the whole of creation.

As a Christian and as one called to the sacrament of holy orders by the Roman Catholic Church, I have the obligation and privilege to be a preacher.[22] I am called to walk with people on this journey of life, and on this journey I will plumb the experiences of my life and of those with whom I live my life here in western North Dakota. In the end, my prayer is that I will be in right relationship and assist others in establishing right relationship in their own lives.

---

[20] See Robert Coles, 'Some Thoughts on Religious and Spiritual Education with Vulnerable Youth', in Coles, *et al.*, *The Ongoing Journey Awakening Spiritual Life in At-Risk Youth* (Boys Town, NE: Boys Town Press, 1995).

[21] See André Resner Jr, *Preacher and Cross: Person and Message in Theology and Rhetoric* (Grand Rapids, MI/Cambridge, UK: William B Eerdmanns, 1999), 140-41.

[22] '... priests, as co-workers with their bishops, have as their primary duty the proclamation of the gospel of God to all.': 'The Decree on the Ministry and Life of Priests' *('Presbyterorum Ordinis')*, in *The Documents of Vatican II*, ed. Walter Abbott, trans. Joseph Gallagher (Piscataway, NJ: New Centuries, 1966), 538-39.